Life Takes Wings

Praise for *Life Takes Wings*

"A true story of a woman's drive and intensity, told with humility, grace and humor. *Life Takes Wings* is a great American flying story. In this rendition of Captain Rippelmeyer's flying life, readers will admire the determination, sacrifice, and courage it took to realize her dream."

–**Deborah Douglas**, author of *American Women and Flight, 1940 to the present*, Smithsonian Library

"Captain Rippelmeyer's book is one of the best chronicles of a flying life that I have ever read. She meets turbulence with determination and fortitude, but with a positive approach and a marvelous sense of humor, which seems to be rare these days. *Life Takes Wings* is a definite must-read for anyone wishing to chart a successful career path."

–**Jacqueline Boyd, Ph.D.** Chair, Amelia Earhart Memorial Scholarship Fund, and 99s 2020 recipient of the Award of Achievement for Contributions to Aviation

"A trailblazer tells her story of love and devotion to flying. Lynn's determination and love to fly took an Illinois farm girl to the top of the pilot world flying the largest commercial aircraft, a Boeing 747. Lynn's story details the obstacles on the way and how she overcame them to achieve what everyone told her was impossible. Her shared thoughts and emotions of the wonder, beauty, and amazement of flying are universal and yours to enjoy within these pages. You will be inspired to follow your dreams."

–**Joe Ballweg**, retired TWA flight attendant TWA museum volunteer

"Fascinating story of a remarkable woman. I found *Life Takes Wings* to be an easy read with real pilot info, facts, and placement reminding me of works by Ernest Gann and Kerry McCauley. It's a fun book to take along when you're on the road – or in the air."

–**Captain Todd Stokke**, United 737 Captain

"Lynn Rippelmeyer achieved what they said could not be done. *Life Takes Wings* gives a peek into the private, even secretive, life of the men-dominated aviation industry. Even as a lifelong professional pilot of fighters and commercial aircraft, I was surprised to find what sometimes happens behind the closed cockpit doors. Through her humor and openness, Lynn shares with us what it takes to reach a goal. What a powerful, gutsy woman she is!"

–**Captain Shawn Mack**, LtCol USAF, Operational Ready in F15, A10, F16, Check Airman and FFDO on A320, A330, B757, B767, B787 Instructor at Northwest Airlines (retired)

"The epic story of taking advantage of every opportunity as it presents. Told as if her life was a series of chance events, Captain Lynn Rippelmeyer also unblinkingly recalls the struggles which she faced in an aviation world not ready to accept her or any woman in the commercial pilot seat. As a colleague at Seaboard World Airlines, I found Lynn's achievements to be the result of her extraordinary diligence, efforts, talent, and character. Her book is well worth reading."

–**Capt. Ken Kahn**, Webmaster for Seaboard World Airlines

"This book is a great read for the pilot and non-pilot alike. Lynn's intriguing life story is one of perseverance and determination, while using the law of attraction. Lynn forged through a world that was believed to be for men only simply because she loved to fly. She approaches life with a joy, vigor, and not a hint of ego. This book is not only about being the first female 747 pilot, but also how life is a wonderful adventure if you decide to make it so. Lynn's life adventure is one you will not want to miss!"

–**Jere Gardner**, retired air traffic controller

"*Life Takes Wings* reads like a good friend telling you a story over the kitchen table. I felt I was with Lynn as she left her home and family to enter the field of aviation – first as a flight attendant and then as a pilot. The reader feels a part of her life decisions, challenges, and triumphs, and wants to see where each page leads. You come to know Captain Rippelmeyer as the take-charge, adventurous, humble, caring, compassionate person she is —just Lynn."

–**Fay Ross**, Paraprofessional, friend, Waterloo, Illinois

"This book was difficult to put down! I have known Lynn since 1979 when she joined us at the second ISA (International Society of Women Airline Pilots) convention. Sharing the same generation of pioneer airline pilots, we thirst to learn of our respective backgrounds.

Reading *Life Takes Wings*, I became totally engrossed in learning about Lynn's journey from an Illinois farm girl to the first woman to fly a B-747 at a time when such a trek certainly seemed unattainable. Her recollection of details makes this an incredible read. She is an exquisite writer, and her story is delightful!

I highly recommend letting her share her arduous climb to the top of the airline world with you."

–**Captain Beverley Bass**, American Airlines B-777 (retired) Female pilot featured in the Broadway musical *Come From Away*, Winner of Best Musical across North America, Canada, United Kingdom, and Australia Author of *Me and the Sky: Captain Beverly Bass, Pioneering Pilot*

LIFE TAKES WINGS

LESSONS LEARNED BY THE
WORLD'S FIRST FEMALE 747 PILOT

CAPTAIN LYNN RIPPELMEYER

NEW YORK

LONDON • NASHVILLE • MELBOURNE • VANCOUVER

Published in New York, New York, by Morgan James Publishing. Morgan James is a trademark of Morgan James, LLC. www.MorganJamesPublishing.com

Life Takes Wings, a memoir, reflects the author's present recollections of experiences over time. Some names and details have been changed to protect the identity of those involved. Some events and time frames have been compressed, and dialogue has been recreated based on the author's memory.

Printed in the United States of America. Proudly distributed by Ingram Publisher Services.

Morgan James
BOGO™

A **FREE** ebook edition is available for you
or a friend with the purchase of this print book.

CLEARLY SIGN YOUR NAME ABOVE

Instructions to claim your free ebook edition:
1. Visit MorganJamesBOGO.com
2. Sign your name CLEARLY in the space above
3. Complete the form and submit a photo
   of this entire page
4. You or your friend can download the ebook
   to your preferred device

ISBN 9781631957352 paperback
ISBN 9781631957369 ebook
Library of Congress Control Number:
2021944607

Cover Concept by:
Susan Engbring

Cover Design by:
Christopher Kirk
www.GFSstudio.com

Interior Design by:
Chris Treccani
www.3dogcreative.net

Morgan James is a proud partner of Habitat for Humanity Peninsula
and Greater Williamsburg. Partners in building since 2006.

Get involved today! Visit MorganJamesPublishing.com/giving-back

This book is dedicated to the many who:

- had complete confidence in my abilities
- pushed me beyond my comfort zone
- stepped into the teacher role to allow me to learn
- set an example for the kind of person I wanted to be
- showed up as a guide at just the right place and time
- listened, shared, laughed, and cried with me along the way
- played a supporting role in my life stories.

And, to my sons, Lucas and Scott.

TABLE OF CONTENTS

ACKNOWLEDGMENTS

Crew Resource Management, or CRM, is a concept in aviation stating that a team effort is far more effective—and fun— than a lone-wolf, know-it-all dictator. I fully subscribe to this belief as a pilot, a human being, and an author.

I had a supportive crew who felt I had a story worth telling with me on every leg of this memoir's journey. Their combined knowledge, opinions, and insight helped make the creation of this book a fun, shared experience.

The crew manifest includes:

Friend and poet, Hallie, who started the adventure by signing us up for a memoir writing class. Other memoir classmates included John, Denise, Dorothy, Rob, and Ida.

Bill Moseley, who listened, recorded, and wrote about these stories.

Non-pilot family and friends who loved me enough to read the drafts and respond honestly: Daniel, Terre, Fay, Terrie, Paula, David, Judy, Joe, Susan, and Yvonne.

Pilot friends who were invaluable with their input to keep the airplane and flight descriptions authentic: Ken, Tim, Jere, Shawn, Rob, Camp, Karen Kahn.

Dear friend, Dr. C.C., Content Consultant, who joined me weekly for years of edits, rewrites, shared memories and laughs.

Hallie, Dorothy, Karyl, and Donna who read, reread, and edited my writing.

Publishing team: Chriss, Shaun, Olivia, Paula, Ruthlynn

Book cover designer and friend Susan Engbring

Thank you, Crew.

Without your thoughtful caring, time, and energy this project would have never taken flight.

PREFACE

The 747 and I share a unique era in aviation history. Both of our flying careers span the years from early 1970s through 2010s.

My first flight as a flight attendant was on TWA's new 747 in 1972. Serving food and drink to the pilots ignited my desire to sit in a pilot's seat and fly that plane, an impossible dream at the time. However, the mental image kept me striving for the next license and rating throughout my training as a civilian pilot—first in a seaplane, and then land planes in Miami. Flying a Twin Otter and working as a TWA flight engineer helped me get closer to my dream, which finally came true in 1980.

I was hired by Seaboard World Airlines as a 747 first officer and became the first woman to fly the beautiful machine, the Jumbo Jet. In addition to flying lessons, I learned many life lessons along the way. This memoir tells the stories within that journey with hopes that it may help others' dreams come true.

INTRODUCTION

"How would you like to be the first woman to fly the 747?"

Captain Hirschberg pointed to the desktop model of the biggest, most beautiful plane on Earth. How often I had imagined that very thing. I could think of nothing more exciting than to be at the controls; to fly seven miles above the earth with a one-hundred-eighty-degree view of land, sea, and sky; to take off with four powerful engines creating enough speed to lift a near-million-pound machine into the air; and to bring her back to earth smoothly and safely.

As a TWA flight attendant in the 1970s, I had been in awe of the magic happening in the cockpit where I served the pilots. After years of flying lessons and smaller plane experience, I was hired as a TWA Boeing 727 second officer, transferring from the cabin to the cockpit. However, my pilot peers told me women could never fly "the heavies," and I would never be allowed in the captain's seat.

Wondering if his question was sincere, I asked, "Isn't it too much for a woman to handle?"

"It's hydraulics! I'll show you," was Hirshberg's response.

Following through with his offer changed my life.

1

Yes, I Can

"Engine failure, number four."

I heard the call-out as the Boeing 747 roared down the runway for takeoff, going too fast to stop before its end. Red warning lights flashed on the cockpit panel, confirming the right outboard engine was dead. As the huge plane veered off centerline, I pushed hard on the rudder pedal to bring the jumbo jet's nosewheel back to the white stripe. With two engines at takeoff power on one side and only one on the other, it took all the strength I could summon to keep us going straight. Continuing to correct for the uneven thrust with my foot, I pulled back on the yoke to lift the big jet into the air.

I scanned the instrument panel to ascertain our situation and heard Captain Hirschberg to my left call out.

"Positive rate."

Leaving the runway below, I responded.

"Gear up."

After climbing to 800 feet, I released back pressure on the yoke to decrease the rate of climb and accelerated to a safe maneuvering speed. I continued with the checklist's commands.

"Flaps 10. Set max continuous thrust. Start the Engine Failure-Fire checklist. Tell tower we had an engine failure, want a straight-out departure, and need to return. Request the longest runway in use."

The 747 was such a sweet machine. With four engines and multiple backups for every system, an engine failure wasn't considered an emergency—only an "abnormal" situation. However, that didn't minimize the amount of training, planning, coordinated effort, and strength it took to bring the plane back to earth safely.

Reaching our assigned altitude, my crew and I completed the checklists that walked us through our abnormal event and prepared us to land. The crew that evening included Captain Hirschberg in the left seat and Fred at the engineer panel. The check airman, John, was in the jump seat, observing my performance.

After the engine failure, I trimmed the rudder to give my leg some relief during the climb. Reducing power when we leveled off helped as well. Fortunately, we were light and would not have to dump fuel to prevent an overweight landing.

Assured that we had the situation under control, I instructed my captain to tell tower we were ready to return and called for the engine-out descent and approach checklist. I had maintained a slow maneuvering speed with flaps at 10 degrees and stayed close to the airport. With calm winds, we could turn and enter a dog-leg base to the final approach for the requested runway. The engine instruments looked different with three engines doing the work of the usual four, but all else was going well. I intercepted the localizer and descended down the glideslope, making the callouts.

"Gear down. Landing flaps and checklist."

"Remember to use only inboard reversers," Fred quietly reminded me before saying, "One thousand feet."

The practiced response, "Zero rudder trim," came out of my mouth automatically as I prepared to hold the rudder pressure with my foot again. Fred reached forward to turn the rudder trim wheel to zero. We worked together, so the pressure was transferred smoothly to my foot, and I could stay on heading. I was thinking about how well we had done when Captain Hirschberg called out,

"Truck on the runway! Go around!"

I pushed three throttles to near max power to initiate the go-around procedure. Adrenaline flooding my system helped press the rudder pedal nearly to the floor to compensate for the uneven thrust and maintain runway heading.

"Set go-around power," I called as I pulled back on the yoke to climb and once again went through the after-take-off procedure.

My commands were through clenched teeth as my crew-members worked with me to execute the missed approach, and I attempted to keep the big plane going straight. It was a relief when we got to assigned pattern altitude where I could reduce the power and lessen rudder pressure. Although the cockpit air was cool, I was sweating as I reached for the trim wheel to give my leg a break.

The flight engineer's words caught me by surprise.

"Engine failure, number three."

Instead of the much-needed relief, I felt the plane suddenly yaw, demanding even more rudder—a lot more rudder—to go straight. I watched another engine's dials wind down and more warning lights come on. There was no time to be surprised. I had to act.

I pushed the rudder pedal as hard as I could to stop the plane from turning. I had to straighten my leg and lock my knee and hip into position with my body pressed into the back of the pilot seat.

This was considered an emergency—two engines out on one side. It was also a scenario I had been told a woman couldn't handle, and the reason there were no female 747 pilots—and never would be. Although the situation had never happened in the real plane, I had seen the emergency procedure in the Denver simulator. But why here and now? Captain Hirschberg had been supportive, and the check airman seemed nice enough. Why would either of them want to embarrass me?

Enough! I scolded myself. *Fly the damn plane!*

I adjusted the two remaining throttles to maintain speed.

"Tell tower we've had a second engine failure and are declaring an emergency. Start the two-engine inoperative approach and landing checklist."

The checklist's review items included some stark reminders: With less hydraulic power, I would have slower flap extension, higher approach and touchdown speeds, no reversers, and a longer landing distance. I had to touch down quickly. A go-around would use flaps position 1. If a third engine failed, the plane could not maintain altitude but could descend to the runway if nearby. I silently hoped there would not be another missed approach or another engine failure.

On the assigned heading, I captured the localizer. "*Small changes—and wait…*" I repeated Capt. Hirschberg's training instructions to myself as I made corrections. The 747 doesn't respond immediately to input, so the pilot must be patient and calm under pressure.

Again, I followed the instruments leading me down the glide-slope. I initially let the speed increase as we descended, knowing the gear extension would cause it to bleed off, decreasing the number of power/rudder adjustments needed. I pushed only the inboard throttle forward when I needed a bit more power—

both techniques taught by Captain Hirschberg. When the thousand-foot call came this time, I realized the rudder trim had been near zero since the last approach—no wonder it was so grueling, and my leg was so tired. By the time we were on final and I was calling for gear, flaps, and landing checklist items, my voice and leg were shaking from frustration and exhaustion.

The approach and landing went well. *Not perfect, but great under the circumstances*, I thought. It seemed to take forever to slow to taxi speed using only brakes. I took the last turn-off at the end of the long runway and called for the after-landing checklist, still wondering, "*Why?*"

After we read the parking and shutdown checklists, John, the check airman, looked at Captain Hirschberg and then me.

"Great work tonight. Let's meet for dinner to celebrate. First round's on me."

I nodded and tried to smile.

Fred unbuckled from his seat and said, "Good job, guys," as he followed John.

I waited until they were gone before confronting my mentor-turned-traitor.

"*Why* would you do that to me?"

Hurt by his apparent lack of loyalty and consideration, I stared straight ahead.

"*Two* engines out? Same side?"

My hands were shaking as I unlocked the safety harness. I put my palms together between my knees to keep them quiet and took a deep breath. My leg still felt as dead as those two engines. I wasn't sure I would be able to stand and leave.

"I'm not having you up there thinking you can't do something you can," he said matter-of-factly. "You're welcome. Congratulations. And next time, use more rudder trim."

Stunned, I turned to look at him smiling at me. I realized then that he had done it for me, removing any doubt in anyone's mind—especially mine—that a woman could fly the 747.

All I could say was "thank you," and I meant it with all my heart.

747 cockpit

Section I:

Flight Attendant Days

2

The Boys in the Cockpit

The in-flight supervisor looked over the cabin crew of fourteen flight attendants gathered in first class for our briefing. A glance assured her that each of us met the weight-to-height and grooming requirements and had our updated manuals in hand. She read aloud the information the flight deck had given her.

"The captain said flight time is seven hours; flight should be smooth for the most part; weather at Heathrow is foggy, as usual. We are close to a full flight with over three hundred passengers. First-class is full."

Flipping a page on her clipboard, she continued.

"We will choose workstations in seniority order." Then, with a nod to me, she added, "Lynn already offered to work the cockpit and first-class. I assume no one objects."

Those with less seniority smiled and waved their thanks.

The supervisor proceeded to call out names as each flight attendant chose her position. She looked up from the clipboard to continue with her instructions.

"Do the safety checks. They're loading the galleys now. Let me know if anything is missing or out of limits. We start boarding in fifteen minutes. Have a good flight. Remember, a smile is part of your uniform," she said without pausing between sentences or smiling.

With the briefing over, we left the first-class area of TWA's 747 to go to our stations. I was glad to be back after six months away on an educational leave to finish my degree at the University of Illinois.

"I'll help," Carole said under her breath as we walked away together. "That was nice of you to offer to deal with the boys in the cockpit, but why? We have a year of seniority now. Leave it to the newbies. You feeling all right?"

We were classmates as newly hired flight attendants at TWA's Breech Training Academy a year earlier and remained friends.

"It's okay." I smiled and shrugged. "When we were the most junior, I had to work up there. I started asking questions about the plane and flying to deflect the crude comments. Lo and behold, interesting adult conversations were possible! I learned a lot, and I loved the view. It's worth the potential hassle, and I can proba-bly handle it better now than the ones just out of training—you know, taking one for the team."

"Well, better you than me," Carole said as she went into the galley to check that catering had brought everything needed for the elaborate five-course meal we would be serving. I checked the emergency equipment and slides at the doors in the first class cabin before heading up the winding staircase to look in on the pilots.

I entered the cockpit filled with dials, switches, knobs, and levers to see three military haircut heads turn in unison to greet me.

"There she is."

"What took you so long?"

"Our girl for the flight."

"How ya doin' tonight?"

They took turns with their versions of a welcome and then quickly went to "fun" mode.

"Hey, we're playing a little game and placed bets. We need your help to decide who wins. What's your bra size?"

Great, I thought, *it's going to be one of those nights.*

I just shook my head. Flight attendant training didn't include a course on "Dealing with the Cockpit." In 1973, the term sexual harassment had yet to be coined. "The girls" were considered waitresses in the sky and fair game for in-flight entertainment for the pilots. I quickly discovered it was up to me to create and maintain a professional work environment and define acceptable behavior. However, if the pilots refused to act appropriately, there was no recourse other than limiting the time spent with them.

"You all lose. I don't wear one. Not enough to bother."

It was my practiced comeback. I had heard it all before. When I first started, the rude remarks, inappropriate pranks, and crude jokes by men old enough to be my father caught me by surprise, making me blush and stutter. However, to enjoy the surreal views from thirty-thousand feet outside their windscreen and to understand the mystique of what they did, I had to learn how to handle the boys.

"If you want coffee, meals, and drinks, you'll have to behave," I said with a smile but hoped they took it to heart.

"Oh, she's going to be a tough one."

"I guess we better behave—or what?"

It seemed we were still in a boy/girl flirty place. It didn't help that some of the girls liked the inappropriate attention, which encouraged it to continue. Finding a pilot or wealthy passenger to marry was the hoped-for happy ending to their jobs.

I tried an even, flat tone, hoping to start something close to a respectful exchange. "This is my first flight back after an educational leave and teaching in inner-city Chicago. I've handled worse than you guys." My mock-stern expression turned to a smile. "Now, how do you want your coffee?"

"Black."

"Sweet, like you."

"Normal, darlin'."

I had to ask. "New York normal black, Midwest normal with milk, or Southern normal with milk and sugar?"

"Milk and two sugars." His accent should have been a clue.

When I returned with the coffees, I found the guys busy listening to the latest enroute weather reports and our clearance— the route of flight that would take us across the Atlantic. I found it interesting and listened to all the information as I silently handed them their cups. With everyone acting more businesslike, when it got quiet, I ventured a question.

"What's our coast-out point and time tonight? If we're done downstairs, and you don't mind, I'd like to come back."

All three turned in their seats to stare at me. They looked like I had disclosed the secret fraternity handshake. "Coast-out point? Where did you hear that?"

"Other crews told me about it when I was up here admiring the lights along the northeastern coast. I always thought we headed over water immediately leaving New York, but we follow the coastline for hours. It's beautiful. They explained that the point where we leave the coastline and head out over the Atlantic Ocean is the coast-out point."

The other two looked at the captain, who said, "Sure. We love the company anytime. We're routed over Halifax and St. John's, so you'll be able to see lights for about two hours after takeoff."

"Thanks," I said as I turned to leave. Then, to make sure the rules of conduct were clear, I added, "But don't try that trick with the finger wiggling through the empty cup in your lap. I've seen it. Gross."

They were all laughing as I closed the door. It might be a good flight after all.

First day as a TWA Flight Attendant

3

The Gift of Independence

I stepped out of the cockpit, leaving the door open to the first-class lounge, a unique feature of the jumbo jet, the whale, or the Queen of the Skies—all nicknames for the huge plane. It was the practice in those pre 9/11 days to leave the cockpit door open until takeoff. Passengers could climb the circular stairs to peek into the cockpit, chat with the pilots, and even take pictures.

The Boeing 747 brought a new level of sophistication to air travel when Pan Am and TWA flew their first commercial flights in 1970, providing around-the-world-service for the first time. Boeing's latest creation was the largest civilian plane built, with an upper deck for the cockpit and lounge area reached by a now-iconic spiral staircase. Most major airlines had a small fleet of the big planes, and they competed to outfit those first-class lounges upstairs. In the early seventies, they were equipped with standup bars, plush armchairs around cocktail tables, even baby grand pianos!

Descending the spiral staircase to the galley below, I was grateful for the new Stan Herman Safari uniform that had replaced Valentino hot pants and go-go boots we wore the year before. The longer skirts and pantsuits were colorful, comfortable, and much less revealing—indicative of women's changing role and the fading "stewardess" image of glorified waitresses in the sky.

Being a flight attendant was gradually becoming an acceptable career path for both women and men. Our training class in May 1972 included one of the first males, causing the term "stewardess" to be replaced with "flight attendant" and the uniform to be more modest and unisex. The passengers didn't seem to have a problem with a male in the role, but some pilots made homophobic comments. A class of "returning mommas" finished recurrent training after winning a wrongful termination lawsuit for being forced to quit when they became pregnant. A maternity leave option was now part of the contract. Women could now serve as purser to oversee money on board, a position previously entrusted only to men. However, on layovers, male flight attendants, like pilots, got single rooms while "the girls" still had to share. With some effort, the union's representatives broke away from AFL/CIO to create our own union, Independent Federation of Flight Attendants (IFFA), to better negotiate our own contracts. Male and female flight attendants alike wanted a viable career choice and to be treated with respect for the service and safety they provided.

In every phase of flight, we attempted to give our first-class passengers a luxurious experience in the confined space seven miles in the air. Before they boarded, we placed fresh flowers in a crystal vase on the center console lined with white linens. As passengers arrived, I guided them to their seats, stowed their luggage, took their coats, returned with their claim check, and took their drink orders. Once they were comfortably settled, I served them a cocktail of their choosing and warm nuts.

After takeoff, we continued the lavish first-class service by covering tray tables with white starched linen cloths upon which were placed china, crystal, and silverware. We handed out warm, lemon-scented, moistened hand cloths for freshening up and then promptly collected them. In flight, we served cold appetizers, followed by warm ones, with more cocktails, wine, and beer. Large menu booklets announced the five choices for the day's entrée and the order of service for the multi-course meal. As the flight attendant working the aisle took everyone's order, the "galley girl" was busy working the ovens. Organization and timing were essential to ensure foods were placed in the ovens in the correct order, at the right time, and for the correct duration.

The extensive first-class menu offered a variety of choices with each course. Salad was served before the main course going east, but after the meal on the return flight, following the European tradition. Warm rolls were continuously offered from a decorative basket. A larger basket held a selection of wines. The main entree options included snapper almondine, chicken cordon bleu, vegetarian pasta, lamb chops, pork loin, and the signature rib roast carved seat-side. We served a variety of starches and vegetables from a steam cart, stopping at each row to carefully spoon the selected items onto passengers' plates. To finish, we presented a fresh fruit and cheese platter, pastries, ice cream sundaes with toppings, and a coffee service complete with the liqueur of choice. It amazed me that in just a few hours on the overseas flight, these same people could also put away an equally sumptuous breakfast.

Flight attendants in coach were just as busy. Two aisles allowed over three hundred passengers to easily fill the row of ten seats across in four aft sections of the monstrous plane. Coach was divided into four sections of vastly different sizes, making service a challenge. Those working in the galleys coordinated their ovens, and the servers delivered meals to the passengers quickly so everyone could finish about the same time. The movie that followed the meal was shown on large screens at the front of each section, and all four screens had to start simultaneously. Those wishing to watch the show purchased large Y-shaped gray plastic headsets that plugged into the armrest. The movie was the only form of entertainment available.

While looking after the passengers, I gave the pilots the same first-class meal options and service. Each time I went to the cockpit, I got to spend a few minutes enjoying the view. Knowing I was interested, the pilots showed me the map, or "chart" in aviation-speak, the route we had been assigned, and our progress. I found it all fascinating and the resulting interaction much more enjoyable. I left when the conversation switched to the usual three S's—sex, salary, and schedule.

With the meal service over, pilots and passengers happy, the cabin crew could finally eat. Plenty of food was still available. In turn, flight attendants from coach who preferred the first-class cuisine over the three coach options came forward and filled a plate to enjoy in their respective cabins.

Looking at the options laid out on the galley counter, I remembered with a smile that this is where I learned the meaning of *prosciutto, almondine,* and *cordon bleu,* that lamb chops wore little green foil tassels, how to properly uncork champagne, and what wine paired best with each entrée. It was all new and exciting information for a farm girl from Illinois. I loved my job, the people, and all I was learning. Like Dorothy in the Wizard of Oz, sometimes I felt like a tornado had transported me to a different world.

Finding a quiet, private place to relax and eat was a challenge for flight attendants on the 747 because our jump seats faced passengers. The only place out of the passengers' view was behind the galley curtains. To create seats, we pulled out the foot-high metal tray carriers from their storage spot beneath the counter and covered them with blankets.

Carole and I closed the curtains to the first class galley to finally get some food and time to ourselves. Seated on the blanketed metal carriers, we balanced our meal trays on our knees to eat food left from the service, our version of first-class dining.

"Welcome back," Carole said when things were finally calm and quiet enough to talk. "Where have you been? I haven't seen you in months."

"I went back to the University of Illinois to complete my degree. When I got hired here, the interviewer said that after working for six months, I could have an educational leave to finish my last semester, so that's what I did. I was a semester ahead, so I got to graduate with my class of '73."

"What's your degree in?" She asked between bites of salad.

"English education and psychology."

As a child growing up on a farm, my first plan was to be a cowgirl like Annie Oakley and Dale Evans or a farmer like my dad. I loved following him around, asking questions, learning all I could about farm animals and crops. I'm not sure if it was because I reached a certain age or because my brother was born when Mom deemed tagging along with Dad was an inefficient use of my time and his attention. Bugging pilots to teach me about flying reminded me of times spent with my dad. So far, most had been very accommodating and happy to help me understand the mysterious working of the cockpit.

However, in 1973, neither farming nor flying were career options for me. I knew my choices to be teaching or nursing. If I wanted to work for an airline, it would have to be as a flight attendant. I was in the top ten percent of my high school graduating class and could get a teaching scholarship, which was essential as the oldest of four children, all bound for college. Two of my three wonderful aunts were teachers, which helped me decide to be a high school English teacher and undercover counselor. I thought I'd get to see into kids' heads when they wrote assignments and then be equipped to help them with their issues.

"You ever teach?" Carole asked.

"Yeah, inner-city Chicago—Wicker Park Junior High. It was one semester during my junior year. While I was teaching, I was also gathering data for my professor, Dr. Landon, who was writing her thesis on nonverbal communication differences among various ethnic groups and their effect in social settings like schools. It was amazing. I got along great with the kids, but not the principal.

"My assignment was a paid work-study student teaching position. They were so desperate for teachers that they were willing to cover a college student's living expenses to fill the position. My students were from Hispanic, Black, White, and mixed backgrounds. Most were from Puerto Rico. They were all in gangs—even the girls. It was a real culture shock for me in comparison to the small rural town where I was raised.

"The school was unlike any I had ever seen. Doors to the outside were padlocked during school hours, and plywood replaced most of the windows. The playground was a cement slab surrounded by the three-story school. Many of my seventh graders were well into their teens because they were repeatedly held back. Not born in the US, they were placed in whatever class matched their age level when they arrived. Then they were punished for not being able to keep up. They weren't allowed to take books home, so homework wasn't an option.

"Their behavior was sometimes unexpected and tough to handle. One day, they sprayed mace in the halls to keep teachers from following them to the playground where they planned to finish a knife fight that a teacher had interrupted.

"I tried so hard. I just wanted them to want to read, to open the world available in books. I stayed up late typing pages from a children's mythology book to mimeograph at school the next morning so they could make their own books—for some the first they ever had. The myths led to great discussions on communities and beliefs. I let them illustrate the pages they read and hung the art on the wall. We sang the poems they wrote to tunes I could play on the guitar. I let them read and discuss the stories in groups to have fun learning."

I finished with what turned out to be the last straw.

"Mr. Turner, the principal, was unimpressed. He said the books encouraged gang activity; art and music could only be done in those classes, which my students hadn't earned; comparing myths to the Bible upset parents; I shouldn't be speaking Spanish, and they shouldn't talk in groups. I was called into his office more frequently than my students."

One day, I saw him grab one of my students and yell, 'Look at me when I'm talking to you!' Later, I tried to explain to Mr. Turner what I had learned in Dr. Landon's educational psychology class. By looking down, the student was showing deference; looking up and into someone's eyes as he ordered was a defiant action. He didn't appreciate my sharing insights and suggestions. They sounded like criticism from a wet-behind-the-ears twenty-year-old who looked sixteen.

Carole listened without interrupting and just shook her head. Finished with the tale and my salad, I stood to place a slice of roast beef and some vegetables on my plate. I completed my answer to Carole's initial question as I returned to my galley seat.

"I had plenty of material to report back to my professor for her thesis, and I received an A for her class. But I wasn't offered a future position at the school. I didn't expect a glowing letter of recommendation either. So, that was the last time I taught."

"Is that why you applied to be a flight attendant?" Carole asked.

"Not really. Remember Debbie in our training class? It's her fault—or credit, really—since it worked out great. Her mom had set up an interview for her to be a TWA flight attendant during the summer after graduation. I was feeling pretty down after my student teaching experience. Debbie wanted company on the car ride to Chicago and asked me to come along. It turns out the interviewer, Fay, was her mom's sorority sister from Delta Gamma, which was our sorority, too. Debbie was hired immediately but turned it down when she found out she'd have to move to New York. To keep her promise of hiring Debbie, Fay hired me so I could keep Debbie company in New York."

"No interview? Really?"

"Well, Fay asked some questions to fill out the application. She liked that I worked through college as a waitress and bartender. I said I would like to travel but couldn't accept the job because I hadn't graduated yet. That's when she told me about the educational leave that I just finished."

I thought my parents would say no to the idea of my leaving school before graduating, but my mom thought it was a great idea. She liked me in summer school or working somewhere over the summers. I knew it would ease them financially as my second sister was entering college, too. Mom may have heard about the travel privileges for family members as well.

Finding such a fun job instead of teaching seemed like a cop-out to me at first.

"Some days, I felt guilty having this much fun and calling it 'work'," I confessed.

"What was it like being back at school?" Carole asked.

Thinking back to my recent dilemma, I responded. "Strange at first—a real learning, growth experience, which is what school is about, but the biggest lesson came courtesy of my mother. My scholarship covered tuition, but not housing. In the past, my folks had paid for my room in the dorm and the sorority house, but they were full. When I asked for help paying rent for an apartment, she told me that because of my bad choices and setting a bad example for my sisters, I was on my own. I assumed she was referring to the Black guy I was dating in New York as my bad choice. Ironically, he's the one who solved my problem by suggesting a student loan."

I grew up hearing my parents' friends tease them about having three girls in four years who would all be in college at the same time. I vowed to graduate early and help however I could. We had excellent teachers in our small town. Like many of my high school classmates, I was able to test and earn one full semester of college credits. My scholarships covered tuition. I spent my summers in summer school or working at a resort on Mackinac Island. Working at the campus bar helped cover expenses during the school year. The teaching work-study program paid all my fees. I hoped leaving to be a flight attendant before my youngest sister started college helped relieve their burden a bit. No one ever mentioned if they noticed or appreciated the help.

I finished my answer to Carole's question. "A counselor helped me pick out the classes that would allow me to graduate. Bub gave me my job back at Chances R, where my picture as the winner of a bikini contest still hung above the bar. Salary, tips, and the student loan gave me enough to pay the rent and have some left over to buy my first car, a Toyota Corolla—which I drove here, so it all turned out great!"

Carole looked skeptical. "It's all good with your folks?"

I shrugged. "I guess so. I thought she meant I was disinherited or cut off from the family, so I didn't contact my sisters while we were at school—sad because it was our only semester there together. But when I went home for Christmas, everything was normal. No one said a word about it or asked any question about how I managed. My traumatic experience was evidently a non-event for them. When I brought it up later in front of people, Mom said she guessed they owed me, but I'm not counting on it. I'm taking it as an unintentional best-gift-ever—the gift of independence."

Carole was smiling. "Good way to look at it. It's like in all the stories—a person, kid, hobbit, or whoever is alone on a journey and meets obstacles. If the person has good intent and is on the right path, guides appear with gifts and solutions to allow the journey to continue. You must be on the right path."

"And what about you?" I asked her to change the subject.

"I've been here, doing this," she said, waving at the galley. "It's all I've ever really wanted. I'm senior enough to be off reserve, but I like the variety of destinations, and I can get the time off I want. I've enjoyed living in the city. But Donna, a friend from home who flies for Delta, recently asked if I wanted to move to Long Island with her when my lease is up. It's not as convenient without mass transport, but Donna offered to share her car to get to the airport. The beach is really nice during the summer."

Her comments reminded me of my time in the city. "Debbie and I moved into one of those Manhattan 'stew zoos' right after training, too. It was a two-bedroom apartment on 89th and 3rd with four other stewardesses. It was a whole new world to me. More people lived in our apartment building than in my entire town in Illinois. We had a great time getting to know the Big Apple and flying all over the world. When I left New York after six months to go back to school, Debbie was also ready to leave. She quit TWA, returned to the University of Illinois to get her master's degree, and got married."

I placed my tray and dishes into the galley container and came back to the present. "It was great to have the job waiting to return to, but the apartment wasn't available. My boyfriend was kind to let me bunk there, but I have to move soon, too."

"Hey!" she exclaimed excitedly. "If you have a car now, want to move in with us? It would make the rent more manageable, and there's plenty of room."

"Yes!" I responded, matching her excitement and reveling in my good fortune. "That would be fantastic! If it's not too expensive and it's okay with Donna, I'd love to. You're another guide with a gift! Let's get together when we get back."

As I filled three cups with coffee, I said, "I guess I should take the guys their ice cream sundaes and more coffee. I'll be back down in time to prep for breakfast. Or come get me if you need me."

Carole shook her head. "You really like being up there?"

I laughed. "I know it's odd, but it's so beautiful! The guys eventually run out of lousy jokes, have to answer radio calls, give reports, and I ask a gazillion questions to keep their minds on something interesting. Sometimes one of them will even let me sit in his seat when he goes to the bathroom."

I thought they did it to impress me and emphasize why women don't have what it takes to do their job. It did just the opposite. I couldn't see why a woman wouldn't be just as capable.

Before I left the galley, I shared a quick story.

"I tried to sign up for aviation classes this last semester and learn more about what's going on in the cockpit, but the guy at the sign-up table in the armory said they didn't have girls in their class."

"That's a shame," Carole sympathized. "You would have enjoyed it. I guess it's because there are no girl pilots."

She held the curtain for me as I took the first steps up the winding staircase, balancing the tray of coffees and desserts in one hand while holding the handrail with the other.

Carole whispered after me, "I'm fine here on my own. The movie is on for another hour. Go learn about airplanes."

The Farm

Teaching in Chicago

4

A Place by the Water

I was thrilled to accept an invitation to share a house at the beach with Carole and her friend Donna. Getting to know New York had been a wonderful initial experience. Staying in my boyfriend's all-Black neighborhood was culturally interesting, but life on the beach was more me.

Because of the proximity to JFK airport, New York's Long Beach was a popular location for many airline people. It was mid-summer, and something was always happening. Since weekends have no particular meaning to airline employees, there were parties and casual get-togethers any time of day or day of the week. A group gathered each morning to run on the boardwalk. Sand volleyball and other beach games were usually in progress and looking for players. We could enjoy open-air restaurants and bars while barefoot and in swimsuits. Life was good.

International flights originated from JFK, so I chose those over domestic flights, which required a longer commute to La Guardia Airport. I loved exploring all the European capitals on our layovers. I still worked the cockpit, dodging offensive comments while bugging the pilots for more information.

Usually, the flight engineer, or F/E, was the youngest and most willing to give answers. His workstation was next to the jumpseat, where I could sit, watch, and talk. Over the summer, I learned about the various systems—electric, hydraulic, pneumatic, air-conditioning, and fuel—all monitored and controlled by the panel he faced. I found it fascinating that the turning of the engine was the source of power that made everything work inside the plane as well as its propulsion.

One flight engineer took the time to draw a diagram of a wing and explain Bernoulli's principle: an airfoil has a curved upper surface that makes the air flow faster than the air below, which causes lift. Then he took me along on the walk-around, the visual inspection of the plane. He pointed out that the wing and tail were airfoils that allowed the plane to turn and climb.

"The hinged parts at the back of each wing are ailerons," he said, pointing to the B-747's massive wing. "They work together, one going up while the other goes down, to make the airplane roll." He put his arms out with one hand turned up and the other down to demonstrate.

"The tail has the other two airfoils, the horizontal and vertical. The horizontal has the elevator to make the plane pitch up and down; the vertical has a rudder to let it yaw left and right. And, of course, the big tube that everything is attached to is the fuselage."

Walking by the engine, I pointed to it, trying to be funny, and said, "And that's an engine."

"Actually, that's the nacelle or cowling, the engine's housing. The engine is inside," he corrected me kindly. He pointed to the aft part of the nacelle. "See that crack? That part opens up after landing when we activate the reversers. We call them clamshell doors because they come together from each side to make the exhaust and thrust go forward instead of backward." He moved his hands to illustrate the doors coming together. I stopped trying to show how smart I was. Back on the plane, I made a drawing to label the parts so I wouldn't forget.

My education, fun time flying, and life at the beach came to a sudden halt that winter with a pilot strike. Our meager pay went to zero. To add to the problems, we discovered our fabulous summer house was not so great in the winter. It had no heating system or insulation, and the fireplace was only ornamental.

I applied for a New York teaching certificate and found jobs substitute teaching. I also found work bartending at some of the local watering holes. Frequented mostly by police and firemen, I learned a lot about Irish traditions and celebrations, which include lots of drinking. It was going well until the principal where I was teaching found out I was bartending. He told me it set a bad example and I had to choose between my two part-time jobs.

My roommate Donna had returned to a previous job working onboard a sailing yacht that docked in the Boston area during the summer and in Antigua, British West Indies, during the winter. The boat's owner, Sumner Long, sent friends to enjoy his boat and the islands during the winter. His Boston crew not only maintained the boat and sailed it to Antigua, but they also played host to Mr. Long's guests. The crew included Captain Jim, first mate Skip, and cook/second mate Donna. Donna called from Antigua, saying they needed help. I was glad to come to the rescue. The free flight benefits TWA gave employees as compensation for no work or paycheck came in handy, so I could fly to Antigua.

The cab ride from the airport on the north shore to English Harbour on the opposite side of the island gave me my first glimpse of a Caribbean island and lifestyle. A delight to all the senses. brightly colored houses gave neighborhoods the look of a box of a crayons. Lovely sing-song accents made the dark-skinned locals' version of English sound more like music than language. The air held a heavy dampness that smelled of salt and lush greenery. I loved the warm sunshine of the tropics on my face and the wind in my hair as we drove with windows down along the bumpy roads. How extra sweet remembering it was January in New York!

Donna met me at the harbor's main entrance and gave me the grand tour. Each boat had a unique name and home port painted on its stern. She explained that boats are named and considered feminine. I realized I had a lot to learn about boats and sailing—just as I had with planes and flying.

Donna introduced me to our boat and home, *Aquarius*. She was a yawl, a sailboat with two masts, seventy-three feet long, with an aluminum hull. Donna explained that the yacht was narrower and lighter than most boats her length because she was built to win races, which she famously did in the 1960s under the name *Ondine*. All of that was lost on me. Growing up on a farm, I had never been on the ocean or a sailboat. I knew as much about a yawl or ketch as the captain did about a John Deere or McCormick.

My new mates were a pleasant lot, in their twenties, attractive and fit from spending their days in the sun and sea air. Over dinner the first evening on the boat, they took turns explaining the situation and our job.

"The wealthy owner used the boat for racing in the sixties. Now, he sends groups of four to eight friends who want to sail from Antigua to the other islands."

"We go south to Montserrat, then Guadeloupe, Dominica, and Martinique."

"Each island is a day's sail from the next, so it makes for a great seven-to-ten-day vacation."

"At night while the guests sleep, we take turns at the wheel. It will be nice to have your help once you get comfortable."

"It's great sailing under the stars. You'll love it."

"They get breakfast and dinner on board unless they decide to eat in town. They spend the day touring the island and shopping. We get to go exploring!"

"You can also help shop and stock the galley, cook, serve the guests, keep the boat ship-shape."

When my smile disappeared for the first time, Skip quickly added, "With the rest of us, of course," as everyone nodded in agreement.

They loved what they were doing and were glad to have me on board. As third mate and second cook and bottle washer, I quickly fit in. They were patient teachers, and I soon learned the terminology and theory of sailing enough to take orders and truly be of help.

I concluded that as crew, we had the best deal of all. We got to do the sailing under the moon and stars while the guests slept at night. During the day, we had fun exploring each island while the guests toured and shopped. Jim knew the locals, where to get needed supplies, and where to find the best spots to relax.

The island of Dominica was my favorite. There, we followed a trail through a jungle of gigantic versions of my houseplants, vines with gorgeous flowers and huge ferns. The path took us to hot springs, where we enjoyed our spa before continuing to the water-fall. We swam in the pool at the base of the falls and climbed into the cave behind it to dive through a sheet of falling water. It was our private paradise for the day. We returned to the boat in time to prepare hors d'oeuvres and drinks and start dinner for our guests.

After dinner, our guests sat below drinking and chatting while we prepared the boat to set sail. They slept in the staterooms as the wind blew our ship to the next island. The crew offered me one of the bunks below, but I preferred to use cushions from the cockpit as a mattress on deck and a folded sail as cover if needed. The wind and water were right there to hear, see, smell, and feel. I loved watching the stars overhead march across the sky, the gentle rise and fall of the boat over the waves, the sense of connection between the sea's rhythm and mine. When navigating to the next island, we could use a star on the horizon as our guide. The sailboat seemed less of a machine than the plane, more an integral part of nature, moved by the elements. The sailor had to know and respect nature to journey safely. I tried to learn all I could.

Between our chartered excursions, we spent time at dock performing endless repairs and cleaning. Like many fast, beautiful ladies, *Aquarius* demanded a lot of attention and was high maintenance. The to do list was never-ending. However, even Captain Jim followed island time, taking lots of breaks and making even the most mundane projects fun.

One time another boat captain recognized our racing boat, even though she had a different name, and asked for a race. It was thrilling! I'm sure it was nothing like the America's Cup, but it was also nothing like the calm charters. At times, we heeled over so far that the side rail was nearly underwater. We clipped ourselves onto the wire between stanchions for safety as we changed sail positions and direction. It was as close to crossing the line from fun to dangerous that I cared to get. We won and had a great time celebrating with the other crew.

When we were at dock in French Harbour, we were next to a boat named *Immamou,* owned by Ted from Vermont. *Immamou* was wooden, heavy, broad in beam, made to withstand whatever the seas threw at her. Personified, she was the female version of her owner of German heritage, just as I imagined *Aquarius/Ondine* being the "eye candy" for her wealthy New England owner. You can tell a lot about people from their boats.

I liked Ted immediately. His eyes sparkled when he talked, as if he were thinking of a joke to tell or a trick to pull. He did both often and loved being at either end of the joke or prank. He had thick gray hair and a deeply tanned, well-toned body for an "older man" in his forties. His raspy voice was the result of smoking and throat cancer, I would find out later. He always wore khaki shorts, and his feet had deep cracks, making me wonder if he ever wore shoes. He started his days with rum in his coffee and ended it with a rum and tonic.

Because he was alone, we often invited Ted over for drinks and meals. We also helped each other with boat maintenance and daily chores. He gave us lessons in knot tying and celestial navigation. I found a *Pilot Handbook of Aeronautical Knowledge* in his boat library that explained the basics of aerodynamics, which also applied to sailing! Ted, a pilot and a sailor, was glad to answer my many questions about how the two activities compared and shared basic fundamentals.

One day, Ted invited us to join him for his TGA, Ted's Great Adventure. We arrived on *Immamou* to find the galley table covered with vacuum-packed, rust-resistant painted cans of pirate booty and a pile of treasure maps. He liked giving out the maps as parting gifts to his cruising friends, so they could find the stash he left behind. We were to divide up and hide the cans where the X marked the spot on the maps, a treasure hunt in reverse.

We set off as a group, then split up with various destinations for our treasures. One hiding place I will always remember because I almost didn't get out. Along the rocky wall of a cove, I found the cave I thought Ted must have in mind. It seemed pirate-treasure-perfect. It could be entered only by swimming to a ledge and following a narrow path to the cave entrance.

I had a great time exploring and choosing among the many hiding places for the can inside the cave. However, when it came time to leave, it was no longer so perfect. The tide had gone out, so I couldn't just slip into the water and swim away as I had planned. As I watched the waves recede, rocks covered with sea urchins' pointy spikes were exposed. I had been able to swim safely between them before, but now it was going to take a very shallow dive and perfect timing with a wave to exit without getting hurt.

I considered my options. I wasn't sure anyone knew exactly where I was, how long they would wait to look for me, or what they would do if they came, since swimming in was no longer an option. I knew there were two high and low tides each day about six hours apart and that waves came in sets. I tried calculating the next high tide, which was hours away and no help at all. The longer I procrastinated, the lower the tide went and the worse the situation got. I finally concluded I just had to go for it. I watched a few waves come in to imagine the timing I needed and waited for a good strong set of waves that I prayed would keep me safe. I dove in, trying to stay as close to the surface as possible and let the tide pull me out to the deeper part of the cove before swimming to shore. Fortunately, it worked.

When I returned to the dock, we each shared our adventures of the day. Ted explained that he had discovered the cave much earlier in the day when the tide stayed high and had no idea of the potential danger. We agreed that particular can did *not* need a map leading another unsuspecting, ill-timed treasure hunter to it. Days at dock were not supposed to be more dangerous than the ones at sea!

I was enjoying my life on the boat when word came that the pilot strike was over. I was sad to leave my new friends and neighbors in English Harbour. However, after four wonderful months in the Caribbean, I needed to return to New York, TWA, and reality.

Soon after my return, I received a ship-to-shore radio call that I knew could be from only one person. Ted was making his way up the eastern seaboard on *Immamou*. Between his hard-to-understand raspy voice and the poor connection, it was difficult to hear what he was saying. There was something about a "young pup" who was supposed to help him but jumped ship when they got to New York. I understood that he was in Poughkeepsie needing help to get the rest of the way to Vermont. He understood that I would try my best to be there ASAP.

Helping people out had worked well for me in the past, and the timing was perfect once again. I was beginning a stretch of ten days off. Air Vermont, which had its small counter in the TWA terminal at JFK, had flights to Poughkeepsie and gave free rides to TWA employees. I packed that night, caught a flight in the morning, and followed Ted's instructions to find *Immamou*.

I got a cab from the airport to the dock, where I found Ted and *Immamou* waiting for me. Ted explained that the Hudson River with its thirteen locks connected the Atlantic Ocean and Lake Champlain. The passage required two people protecting the boat while the locks filled with water, so my assistance was needed and greatly appreciated. After the last lock, we would enter Lake Champlain and sail home. The home Ted referenced was his two-hundred-acre private island near Burlington, Vermont, called Savage Island.

Immamou

5

Vermont Home, Family, and Flying Lessons

As we navigated the Hudson River on *Immamou*, Ted explained that Savage Island was one of seventy-one islands in Vermont's Lake Champlain, and some were privately owned. Savage initially had been a family summer getaway, but it became his permanent residence after his divorce. He planned to spend winters aboard *Immamou* in the Caribbean and summers on Savage.

Ted's girlfriend, Susan, warmly welcomed me to their rustic cabin. Ted had mentioned that he hoped Susan could join him in Antigua when school was out. I assumed it was because she was a teacher, so I was surprised to find she was a student and younger than I was. They met when she was helping with his election campaign for the Vermont General Assembly. He had family money and felt an obligation and civic responsibility to use it to make the world better as a politician. Ted's time in the state legislature resulted in a billboard ban in Vermont.

His time campaigning led to the relationship with Susan. The couple shared the love of boating and island life. Adding sheep to the island was Susan's idea. She used a spinning wheel and loom to spin wool from the sheep, knit sweaters, and make covers for the colder winter days. Withholding judgment about the age difference, I enjoyed getting to know the young woman who proved to be as beautiful inside as she was out.

I had a few days left before I had to be back in New York, so I gladly accepted their invitation to spend the time enjoying the peace and beauty of Ted's island. The grand tour included Sandy Beach, the Cove, Fern Forest, The Copse, The Point, Nature's Trail, Sheep Meadow with barn, The Gardens, and Landing Strip. Yes, the island had its own airplane landing strip. In a previous life, Ted and his former wife both flew planes. In the divorce, she got the house in town; he got the island.

Susan had grand plans for The Gardens. Rows were labeled for various vegetables. Corners were set aside for patches of asparagus, melons, gourds, and strawberries. Volunteer plants from the previous year were popping up with the spring sunshine. Marigolds surrounded the garden to keep out insects. Tall sunflowers stood at one end, with irises, lilies, and other flowers blending among wildflowers. Fruit trees lined the path from the cabin to the garden. Susan explained that they were experimenting with several different apple varieties. Her description was so vivid I could see it too. My gardening grandparents would have been impressed. I loved helping them as a child and offered to help Susan with hers, immediately increasing the possibility for future invitations to the island.

During the tour, I noticed a few things without being told. There was no running water; it was hauled in buckets from the lake to the cabin. Although Ted declared the water of "pure, curative quality," Susan ran it through a filter for drinking. Inexplicably named The Birdcage, the outhouse was situated so that one might enjoy the best view of the lake and opposite shore. It was doorless so that you could do just that. Electrical power came from a few solar panels connected to batteries and a generator. Gas had to be hauled from the gas station onshore in containers on the boat, so the generator was used sparingly. Appliances were hooked to propane tanks behind the cabin. Trips to town were an all-day ordeal, so planning and organization were mandatory—and Ted's specialties. I imagined that living on an island, like being on a boat, made one very aware of everything's source and what impact discarding it had on the environment and nature. I thought it would be good for everyone to see other countries and ways of life and to work on a boat or island for a while. There were so many interesting ways to go through life while taking care of our home planet.

The next morning after breakfast, Ted, Susan, and I took our rum-infused coffees out on the deck to discuss the day's projects and enjoy the delightful weather. There was a lot to do since Ted had been gone for the winter months. Before we had agreed on what to tackle in what order, I heard the distinct sound of a plane growing louder as it came closer. The aircraft suddenly burst into view directly overhead, level with the treetops, momentarily blocking out the sun. Startled, I spilled some coffee as I looked up and instinctively ducked. It was a strange sight, carrying what looked like two large metal canoes where the landing gear should be. The plane rocked its wings and then disappeared behind the trees.

"It's Bill and Dawn!" Susan exclaimed, obviously pleased. I followed her and Ted down the shaded dirt path that led to the cove. By the time we got there, the small, strange craft had completed its landing (if it can be called a landing on the water), shut off its engine, and was silently drifting toward shore. Ted stepped into the water to guide the floating plane onto the sand, careful to miss the rocks. A man and woman spryly hopped out of the doorless plane, using the metal float as a step into the knee-high water. They were both smaller than I and older than my parents—about Ted's age, I guessed. They had the same tanned outdoor skin and athletic bodies dressed in khaki shorts and cotton tops. The woman had short gray hair, a smile, and a cheerful voice that reflected her nature. The man, who took over from Ted getting the plane to shore, was balding and had a drooping shoulder. I learned later he had had childhood polio, but it hadn't slowed him down in the least. They were all very happy and excited to see one another.

I stood off to the side as greetings were exchanged and conversations about familiar people and topics began among them. Dawn and Bill were the first of the many friends and neighbors who would descend upon the island over the next few days.

Eavesdropping allowed me to learn that Dawn and Bill owned a neighboring island, Stave. The couples visited each other frequently. As the friends talked, trading local news and gossip for Ted's latest sailing adventure, my attention was drawn to the craft that looked more like a toy than a real plane. I waded into the water to get a closer look. It appeared to be straddling a pair of closed metal tubes flat on top and pointed at the ends that kept the plane afloat. I learned later they were pontoons, and the plane was a Piper J-3 Cub on floats, a floatplane or seaplane. The wings were on top of the fuselage instead of on the sides. Short ropes that hung down under each wing were used to pull the plane on the water.

I took a peek inside. Instead of a door was a window in two hinged parts. The top half swung up and was held in place with a clamp under the wing. The lower half swung down to lie flat against the outer fuselage, leaving the cockpit completely open. Inside the cockpit were two tandem seats. Short sticks for steering were positioned in front of each seat where a Y-shaped yoke would be on TWA's planes, the only thing I could compare. The Cub's dashboard consisted of only six round instruments and some knobs.

I recognized the instruments, thanks to my recent Q and A sessions with the pilots during flights. I also noticed no navigation or communication radios, no system dials and switches, no flap or gear handles. Just as I had been amazed that something so gigantic as the 747 could actually take off and fly, I was equally impressed that something as small, simple, and fragile looking as this floating Piper Cub could do the same.

I stepped up on the pontoon to get a better look. When I touched the plane's side, I realized it wasn't metal, but a strong coated fabric stretched over a metal frame.

"And that's Lynn, my crew, who I met in Antigua this spring and was nice enough to help get me through the locks."

I heard my name and turned around to see Ted nodding toward me. Feeling like I had been caught trespassing, I jumped off the pontoon into the shallow water and waved at the guests as I started to shore.

"We've invited her to stay a few days before she has to go back to work at TWA," interjected Susan.

"Hi," I said, smiling at the new couple. "I'm sorry if I was nosy."

"It's fine," Bill assured me. Then he surprised me with, "Want to go fly?"

I couldn't believe it. I looked at Ted and Susan to get a sense of etiquette in the unusual situation. They were smiling and nodding.

"Sure! Really? Now?" It was hard to contain my excitement.

"Jump in," he responded, pointing to the front seat. I stepped inside to sit on the small seat with the stick between my knees. Bill pulled on the rope to easily pivot the plane on the water's surface and face into the middle of the lake. The three friends onshore gave us a final push.

Standing on the pontoon, Bill reached inside to move a switch and knob. Turning to the front of the plane, he grabbed the propeller from behind to push it down as hard as he could. After a few attempts, the engine coughed and sputtered to life, causing the propeller to spin and move us across the water. Bill jumped into his seat and pulled the knob back, which caused the engine to go to idle and become quieter. He wiggled the stick, which clearly was connected to the stick in front of me, because it moved, too. Realizing we were not shutting the window/door, I grabbed the seatbelt and tightly buckled it. Bill pushed the knob all the way forward, and the Cub began plowing through the water, the engine giving its all. After a few moments, the seaplane lifted enough to skim across the water's surface. Bill pulled up on a wire on the floor to my left. He later explained it was connected to the water rudder on the back of one of the pontoons, which controlled the plane's direction while on the water. Once we were flying, it was retracted, and the stick controlled our movements. Another wire that poked out of the front cowling just in front of the windshield was the gas gauge! When the top of the wire dropped to the top of the cowling, the gas tank was empty.

The flight instruments indicated that everything was done at sixty knots—climb, cruise, and descent. We climbed up above the lake very slowly, where Bill leveled, and the engine got a bit quieter. It still was much too loud to talk, so I just sat back to enjoy the view—for about two seconds. The engine went almost silent, the stick between my legs came back to the edge of the seat and the plane's nose pointed up to the sky, pushing me back into my seat and showing me nothing but clouds. The little plane shuddered and suddenly fell sharply to the right. My unexpecting body was pushed against the wall, straining the seatbelt. Then the stick went all the way to the left and forward. We were pointed at the water and coming down fast. Bill wasn't acting panicked, so I assumed all was under control and that it was a demonstration of how safe and sturdy the seaplane was. Just before we reached the wet surface below, the plane leveled, gently kissed the surface of the lake, and then, with the engine in full power, climbed again. It was thrilling—like a roller coaster ride.

We made steep turns in S patterns and circles and did climbs and dives while turning. His version of having fun, I thought. Now and again, he would give me a thumbs-up over my shoulder, asking if I was OK. I returned the OK sign with a nod of my head. Back up above the treetops, we followed the shoreline of the island below with its grass landing strip, sheep barn, pasture, evergreen trees and fern forest, the sandy beach, and our friends now relaxing on the log cabin's deck.

I saw the stick moving back and forth quickly in front of me and then Bill's hands up in the air. He turned to point to my stick and then to me. He wanted me to take the controls? To fly? I took the stick in my right hand and gently pulled it to the right. We turned in that direction, and Bill gave me a thumbs-up, so I continued experimenting—left, right, forward, back with the stick as the little plane responded to my requests.

I put the wings level to the horizon. I took time to enjoy the view through the windscreen: tiny cars on the mainland moving silently across the bridge, the sun sparkling on the lake scattered with toy fishing boats, sailboats with colorful spinnakers, field rows ending at the water's edge. I had the same wonderful feeling and a similar view as when I was a girl and rode my horse, Lucky, to the top of the bluffs near our farm in the Mississippi River valley of Southern Illinois. Below us lay a patchwork quilt of green and gold fields stitched together with railroad tracks and streams. Birds glided below our limestone lookout as the breeze held them aloft while blowing Lucky's mane and my hair. I would imagine Lucky sprouting wings like Pegasus to join the birds flying through the valley. This sweet little Cub was allowing that imagining to become real.

I tried turning left and then right, going up and down as Bill had. I loved it. Too soon, the control stick wiggled in my hand again. I let go, reluctantly giving control of the seaplane back to Bill. We went spinning down toward the lake, then flew just a few feet above the water back to the cove where we took off.

With the engine at idle, our speed grew slower and slower until the seaplane splashed onto the lake. I felt the weight of the craft settle heavily into the water, becoming more like a boat than a plane. The lowered water rudder gave us directional control, and our momentum caused us to drift closer to shore. Bill turned off the engine and waited for the prop to stop turning before jumping in up to his knees. He guided my now-favorite plane in the world safely onto the sand. He took a rope from under the seat and expertly tied it to the cleat on top of the pontoon before heading to the nearest tree to tie down.

I unbuckled and reluctantly stepped out to walk the few steps to shore, leaving the floatplane bobbing in the water behind me. Bill looked at me and said, "You okay?" as he searched my face.

I assumed the smile plastered there would have answered that.

"Yeah. Better than okay. That was amazing."

Ted, Susan, and Dawn greeted us inside the cabin with anxious questions. How was it? Where did you go? What did Bill do?

Did you get sick? Did you get to fly? I gathered from the questions, discussion, and expressions that Bill had a reputation for taking young girls up for their first flight and turning it into more of a fright than a flight.

Since I was still smiling and wanting more, Dawn explained that both she and Bill were licensed instructors and needed a student to maintain their certificates. She asked if I would like to continue with lessons during the summer. She later added in confidence that giving flying lessons to me would keep Bill busy. I would be doing her a favor. I could hardly believe it. There was nothing that I wanted more in the world. I explained that I didn't have a lot of money, but they said the lessons were free. It was a dream come true, and it was the only way I would have ever been able to take lessons. To make the dream complete, Ted and Susan issued an open invitation to come back any time to stay at their cabin.

After ensuring both the offer of housing and flying lessons were sincere, I began spending all my free time in Vermont. It became my refuge—my home and family. Ted instigated a fatherly inquisition to any new boyfriend I brought along. We engaged in philosophical and hilarious conversations; he was interested in and valued my opinions. We agreed on almost everything except politics, which we respectfully agreed to leave alone. Unlike my farm family, there were no gender-specific roles. Ted enjoyed teaching me how to do repairs and figure out how things work, and then he helped in the garden and kitchen. Susan was a wonderful sister substitute without any rivalry or jealousy. Dawn started each visit wanting to know how I was, listening attentively to the answer, making me feel safe to share my past, hopes, and worries without a hint of competition, teasing, or bullying. Bill was like the crazy uncle that made families interesting. I grew to care for them as family and knew they felt the same affection for me.

It was a magical summer. As soon as I landed from working a TWA flight, I jumped on Air Vermont to fly to Burlington. On arrival, I went immediately to the airport bathroom, where I changed from city girl flight attendant to country girl island pilot. I replaced stockings, uniform, and makeup with khaki shorts, cotton blouse, and sandals. The mandatory smile was replaced with genuine excitement and happiness.

At the end of each visit, I had to reverse the routine, remove my island attire, and replace it with the Halloween costume of a flight attendant. I looked in the mirror, knowing the real me could emerge the next time I came to Vermont.

Each time I landed in Burlington, the gate agent handed me a cryptic note or puzzle left by Ted, leading me on a scavenger hunt to find car keys. I'd drive to the landing in Grand Isle to see Ted and/or Susan waiting for me. Lake Champlain is twelve miles wide and runs one hundred twenty miles from Canada between Vermont and New York. The boat ride to the island transported me into another world. I could pretend it was a mythical ship taking me to Avalon, the mystical island near Camelot, a place of peace and beauty where I could relax, trust, breathe deep, and be me.

I spent so much time on the island during the summer that I had my own room and a place at the dinner table. Ted and Susan were genuinely glad to have the company and my help with the daily chores and routine of the island. There were the usual household chores, the huge garden to tend, hay to bale, sheep to move from one pasture to another, machinery to repair, and a never-ending to-do list. Evenings were for playing cards, reading, talking about what we were reading, and life in general.

I enjoyed the routine morning dip in the curative waters (according to Ted) of Lake Champlain to heal whatever ails body, mind, heart, or soul. With no running water in the cabin, morning showers were replaced with a morning dip. Armed with soap, shampoo, toothbrush, toothpaste, and towel, we headed to Sandy Beach. The water was so cold in the spring that it was a very quick event. As summer warmed the lake, we added a swim to the morning ritual and dips throughout the day.

Bill or Dawn flew in on the days the weather allowed to give me a flying lesson. Bill owned a strip-casting machine manufacturing plant on the nearby shore of Colchester. He had created a work environment with his employees that allowed him to come and go as he pleased. Dawn, his devoted wife and partner in all things, was capable of going in whatever direction and sharing in any adventure he chose. She was one of the most amazing people I had ever met.

Whenever I heard the Cub's arrival, I stopped whatever I was doing and rushed to the cove. To save time and ensure the pontoons didn't hit rocks near the shore, the Cub stayed in waist-high water. I swam out, climbed aboard, and wrapped in the towel waiting on the seat. At the end of the lesson, I replaced the towel and swam to shore.

In many ways, visits to Savage Island were like going to Neverland. There was a sailboat and island where we were secluded from the rest of the world. Ted, like Peter Pan, was a forever-boy, playing at life. With family money, he had the funds to play sheep farmer and sailor. Susan, like Wendy, was a young girl playing mother and grown-up. Chores, problem solving, and plans were all fun and games. For me, however, learning to fly took a lot more than sprinkling some fairy dust.

Both of my instructors seemed to genuinely enjoy teaching and liked the excuse to play in their seaplane. I insisted on buying the gas, which they allowed. By mid-summer, I had logged forty hours in my little red pilot logbook. I knew all the flying maneuvers by heart, but still loved practicing, improving, and exploring all that the lake had to offer. Aloft, the world looked and felt right. It was peaceful and orderly, but full of adventure and fun. It was where I wanted to be.

On days when we couldn't fly, Dawn gave lessons from the Pilot Handbook to prepare for the written and oral exams I would take if I wanted a private pilot license. All the studying and lessons weren't meant to lead to a career, of course. I knew there were no flying jobs for women. The TWA pilots had explained all the reasons: there was the obvious physical inadequacy—a woman was too small and weak, plus the lack of mental, emotional, psychological wherewithal and abilities. Some male pilot would inevitably add, "And there's that time of the month when she shouldn't leave the house." Except for the last comment, I assumed they must be correct since they were the career experts. If women could be pilots, there would be some, right?

All of that didn't matter at the time; I was just enjoying the fun while it lasted.

In 1973, at age twenty-two, I had found something I loved doing more than I could have ever imagined. I was addicted!

Piper Cub taking off

Lucky, My Pegasus

My love of riding transferred easily to a love of flying

Section II:

Flying Lessons

6

Be Back in 10

It was a characteristic fall day in Vermont that people flock to see, filling the B&Bs and crowding the streets and country lanes with "looky-loos and leafers," as my friends called them. I wanted to enjoy a view of the landscape's colorful displays, but from a different vantage point, the air. The day was clear with light winds, so I had my fingers crossed, wishing for a flying lesson.

Taking advantage of the unseasonably warm day, Susan and I were bringing in the last of the vegetables from the garden to put up for the long winter when I finally heard the sound I had been hoping for all morning—the drone of the Cub's small engine off in the distance. I dropped the zucchini in Susan's basket and ran to the cove where Bill would be landing. As I rounded the corner, I heard the familiar splash of the plane's pontoons touch the lake's surface and the engine slow to idle.

The seaplane, the object of my new obsession, sat waiting for me, bobbing in her wake. I waded the short distance, pulled myself up onto the pontoon with the help of the wing spar, and reached for the towel waiting on the aft seat. I dried off quickly and wrapped it around my still damp body before climbing in. I was a bit surprised to find Bill in the front seat where I usually sat, but Bill was full of surprises, never telling me what the lesson would entail.

The backseat controls were linked and identical to those in front, so flying would be the same—the view just wasn't as good. I placed my feet on the rudder pedals and wiggled the stick between my knees, giving the signal I was ready. I saw Bill retract the water rudder and raise his hands, signaling that he was ready, too. She was all mine.

Smiling to myself and the world in general, I put my left hand on the knob that was the throttle and pushed it forward gently. Already facing into the wind and away from shore, all I had to do was head straight down our water "runway" to take off. With the throttle full-forward, the Cub gradually, very gradually, picked up speed. The 65-horsepower Continental engine was giving its all to overcome the friction of the water on the two Edo aluminum floats. When we eventually reached about forty knots, we unstuck and glided over the lake's surface. At sixty knots, I pulled back firmly but smoothly, as I had been taught, to allow us to rise out of the water. I then leveled the plane for a moment to increase airspeed in ground effect—or in this case, water effect—before pulling back further to cause the nose to rise and initiate a climb. At a rate of only fifty feet per minute, it seemed to take forever to get to the desired altitude of three hundred feet.

Bill signaled to start a slight right climbing turn toward the causeway, a narrow strip of land we often used to practice maneuvers. We had become quite adept at this form of nonverbal instruction. The lessons usually lasted about forty-five minutes, but time seemed to stop as I concentrated on implementing all he and Dawn had taught me over the summer.

Bill's hand was now making a snaking motion, indicating S-turns. With the causeway and the tall towers spaced evenly alongside, it was a perfect place to practice what was called "pole bending" in Western horse shows. After checking the wind's direction in the tell-tale signs in the water below, I wound left, then right, crossing between the towers. The goal was to make 180-degree turns that created a ground track with equal curves around each tower while staying at the same altitude. This maneuver was fairly easy on a calm day, but with the wind, I had to compensate by increasing the bank angle here, decreasing it there to keep the ground track symmetrical. With each try, the pattern became more precise. I hoped Bill thought so anyway. I knew the circling motion his finger made called for turns about a point. Again, compensating for the westerly wind, I tried to fly a perfect circle around one of the towers without losing or gaining altitude. Bill must have thought it was good enough and gave the go-home signal.

I was disappointed that the lesson had been so brief, but that didn't last long. Bill suddenly cut the engine to idle, simulating an engine failure and calling for an emergency power-off landing and bringing all of my attention to the task at hand. I again checked the telltale wind lines on the water below and lined up parallel to fly directly into the wind and touch down at minimum speed. I pushed the nose over to maintain a glide speed of sixty knots until just above the water when I pulled back to flare, stop the descent. Now floating just inches above the water, I continued easing back on the stick to lose more speed. Finally, with insufficient airflow over the wings to keep flying, we touched down in the water. We continued toward Savage Island with the usual series of touch-and-goes (takeoffs and landings in quick succession), pleased that such a large lake was an unending runway.

As we approached the cove, the stick wiggled in my hand, and I let go. Bill took control of the airplane for the final landing, coming in as close to the shore as possible. With the engine at idle, the plane came to a stop, weather-vaned into the wind, and pointed back out to the middle of the lake. Unsure of what he was doing or wanted next, I waited.

He reached over his right shoulder and handed me a small piece of crumpled paper. I smoothed it out on my knee and found the scrawled message:

BE BACK IN 10

While trying to figure out what it could mean, I heard a splash to my right. Bill was treading water! Smiling and waving, he gave the pontoon a final push into the lake.

I was alone in the plane for the first time. No one was there blocking my view out the front window. No one there to tell me what to do next. No one there to catch and correct my mistakes or rescue me in an emergency.

We hadn't discussed this. I hadn't considered it possible. The little plane was Bill's baby. One wrong turn on the water could cause a fatal flip, sending the plane to the bottom of the lake. I hadn't seen anyone except Dawn and Bill allowed to fly her.

He and Dawn must have planned this, I realized. That's why he was sitting in the front. The Cub was flown from the back seat when there was only one person, so if I was going to fly on my own, I needed to be in the back when he jumped out.

Well, if he thought I was capable and ready, who was I to argue?

Besides, what choice did I have? I couldn't jump out and swim to shore, pulling the plane behind me, although the option did come to mind.

I was going to do this.

Alone.

Solo.

Panic and fear are not helpful, I reminded myself, as those emotions arose. Maybe I could pretend to be my own instructor, I thought. I just needed to do what I had done every lesson all summer. To calm myself and get comfortable, I took a deep breath and pretended I had just entered the plane. I went through my preflight routine to make sure I forgot nothing. I rechecked the magnetos, made sure the controls were free, checked that I was headed into the wind and that the water rudder was raised. All with no one there except the instructor—me—to watch or remind the student—me—of anything I missed.

Sitting up as tall as possible to see over the front seat, I pushed the throttle forward. The little plane surprised me by popping right out of the water, much lighter with only me on board. Almost immediately, we were ready to climb. She seemed to like her increased freedom and agility, too.

I climbed to three hundred feet to see the world from way up high, a familiar view after flying here all summer. There were the neighboring islands—Crow's Nest, Fish Bladder, and Stave. To the north, the lake stretched to the Canadian shore, with Montreal too far in the distance to see. On the Vermont side of the lake, the nearest town of Grand Isle looked like an ornamental Christmas village. On the New York shore, fields of newly harvested corn stretched right to the water's edge. Tractors, trucks, and match-box-sized cars were like toys moving silently far below.

Again, I was reminded of my Southern Illinois home and farmlands viewed from atop the bluffs where I imagined soaring over the valley like the birds riding the thermals below. At the same altitude as the bluff's limestone ledge, I flew the seaplane over the fields on the shore. I didn't have to imagine flying any longer. I was doing it!

I used the unobstructed view of the horizon to practice a level three-sixty turn and then pulled back on the power, dropped into a slow descending curve. We were a graceful bird (well, as graceful as a seaplane can be) dropping down to glide just inches above the water before adding power to climb back up again. I flew over Savage, following the ins and out of the island's coves and beaches. In the Cub's open cockpit, cool air blew by me, blue water sparkled below, small white clouds invited me to play. I was in heaven.

I had heard that pilots return from their first solo flight a different person. I wondered if people were aware at such times that a life-changing event was occurring. I wanted this sky and water, this elation, this charged moment to last forever. I envisioned the ranks of my heroes and heroines, those lucky enough to have had this incredible experience—Amelia Earhart, Charles Lindbergh, Dawn, Bill, and Ted, the TWA pilots! Like them, I had soloed! I was a pilot!

I remembered a quote: "Flying encompasses science, beauty, adventure, and freedom. Who could ask for more?" And here it all was. The science of aerodynamics and an internal-combustion engine; the beauty of creation, the adventure of new places, people, sights, and the freedom. Ah, the freedom of flight, escaping the constraints of gravity, space, and time.

TIME!

My ten minutes must be up!

What time was it? How long had it been? Ten minutes? Twenty? Thirty? Where's the clock? How could there not be a clock? What the hell? How could I not have noticed before there was no clock? What about fuel? Panic rushed in.

The bent metal hook, the fuel indicator, was still well above the cowling. Maybe it hadn't been that long. I had been completely calm while time stopped having meaning. Now, with my heart beating wildly and taking short, quick breaths, I banked the plane to find that Savage was just off my right side. Eventually, breathing and heart rate came back to normal. I circled and descended slowly and calmly. I wanted to have room for some landings alone on the way home. Parallel to the wind streaks in the water, I did a series of touch-and-goes. This was so much more fun on my own!

I neared the cove where Bill had jumped out a lifetime ago. I saw him standing on shore with Ted, Susan, and Dawn, who had arrived by boat while I was flying. A final touchdown with the engine at idle brought me near enough to shore to lower the water rudder, turn off the engine, and drift in, just as I had seen my instructors do. My friends stepped forward to guide my plane to a sandy spot beneath the tree used as a tie-down. I stepped out looking the same—but changed. I had soloed. After congratulatory hugs all around, we headed back to the cabin. I began trying to share the experience of what I did and thought and felt.

"That was amazing! Bill, Dawn, thank you so much. I never expected…. It was so much fun. We took off so much easier…. It was just me!"

I was babbling, grinning, talking with my hands, unable to find the right words or finish thoughts and sentences. As pilots, they understood what no words could relay.

It turned out that I was gone a bit more than ten minutes but stayed in sight, and Bill made it safely to shore. Over glasses of sun tea, the three seasoned pilots, Ted, Bill, and Dawn, shared stories of their solo experiences many years earlier, which led to other flying tales of adventure. There never seemed to be a shortage of stories when a group of pilots gathered, but the stories of the first solo were always a favorite. And now I had one, too.

Tradition has it that after soloing, the new pilot's shirttail must be cut off. I have never heard a logical explanation for this widely accepted ritual. I just used the towel.

Winter was coming. I knew my solo would be the last flight of the season, so it was with mixed emotions that I thanked everyone for the best summer and most amazing experience of my life. I couldn't remember being happier or more grateful for a gift—the gift of wings.

Dawn, Bill, and me with Cub on floats

Stave Island, Lake Champlain, VT.

7

Blue Eyes

With the Cub out of the water for the winter, my flying lessons had to end. However, I continued visiting Lake Champlain, where I reached Savage Island by snowmobile or stayed with Dawn and Bill in their shore house. Dawn had become one of my favorite people on earth, a mentor, and whom I wanted to be like when I "grew up." She continued teaching from the Pilot Handbook, which I carried with me to read and study on layovers.

Back at TWA and my flight attendant duties, I continued opting to work first class and the cockpit, to the relief of the more junior flight attendants. When time and personalities allowed it, I bugged the pilots to explain things I didn't understand.

One evening during the boarding process, two young men caught my attention. They appeared to be in their early twenties, one lanky with blond hair, the other stocky with brown-hair. Obviously good friends, they ambled down the jetway with easy athletic strides, chatting and smiling. Sporting jeans, untucked cotton shirts, tennis shoes, and shoulder-length hair, they stood out in stark contrast to the men and women dressed in business attire coming in the first-class section boarding door. Instead of attaché cases, they carried backpacks slung over their shoulder; instead of shiny leather loafers, they wore grass-stained tennis shoes. Positive they were headed to the wrong section, I stopped the first to ask for boarding passes, which confirmed seats 4A and B were theirs. I returned the boarding cards apologetically. The blond guy's direct eye contact, confident smile, and shrug of "don't worry 'bout it" that I got in response took me by surprise. His eyes were a sparkling clear blue with long brown lashes. The handsome tanned face was framed with wavy sun-streaked blond hair curling around his ears, touching his eyebrows and collar. Still kidding around, the two friends looked very much at home as they settled into their seats.

For a change, I was glad to have the multi-course service giving me lots of opportunities to overhear conversations and ask questions plate by plate. By the end of his meal, I had learned "Blue Eyes" was named Sam and his friend was Tom. They lived in Miami as roommates, attended Miami Dade Community College, and were nineteen years old. They had grown up in the Bahamas, where their parents still lived. Both their dads were TWA pilots, and they were using family passes for free travel to London for the weekend. They were hungry and wanted extra of everything. Okay, they finally admitted, it was the end of the month, they were out of funds, the fridge was empty, and the cheapest way to eat was to fly to London for the weekend using Dad's family passes.

They were both friendly, but Sam, sitting on the aisle, did most of the talking. He had a kind, gentle voice that matched his smile and eyes. After the crew removed the dessert plates and second ice cream sundae bowls, we dimmed the lights to allow passengers to sleep or watch a movie. I checked with my coworkers to see if they would cover things while I took a break. At this time, I typically stole away to study, but I noticed Sam's overhead light on. I took one more walk through the cabin and saw him flipping pages in the Pilot Handbook.

"Hey," I said, surprised, and a bit too loudly for other first-class passengers, including Tom, trying to sleep. "What are you doing with that?"

Fortunately, he didn't seem to think the question sounded as dumb as it did to me, or he was expecting the question and was ready with his nonchalant reply.

"Oh, I'm studying to be a pilot," he said, looking up from the familiar handbook, obviously expecting me to be impressed.

"Me, too!" I whispered loudly, kneeling beside his seat.

"What?" he asked, surprised by my response. "What do you mean?" he managed to say after a brief pause.

"I'm studying it, too. I was on my way upstairs to work on it during my break. A friend in Vermont is helping get me get ready for the written exam. She says I'm ready, but I want to make sure I pass on the first try. I took lessons this summer in a seaplane, but the Cub doesn't have the instruments that the book talks about. The 747 does, but it's not easy to learn up there with those guys." I was rambling, and he was staring at me. Tom turned toward the window, trying to go back to sleep.

"Can we go over there to talk?" Blue Eyes asked, pointing to empty seats across the aisle, away from the galley's lights and his friend.

"Sure," I answered, glad for the chance to sit with him.

We spent the rest of the flight leafing through the handbook, comparing notes on what we had learned so far in our flight training, telling stories, sharing our past and hopes for the future. The near dark of the airplane's cabin made it more comfortable to share. Only the soft glow of the wing's navigation light and the moon profiled our faces as we got to know each other.

He planned to become a TWA pilot like his father and older brother. He admitted that competition was tight—the airlines strongly preferred military-trained applicants with four-year college degrees, but he would do all he could to be ready. After community college, he hoped to work as a flight instructor at the school where he presently took lessons. In addition to flying charters, the lessons would allow him to build the hours required by the major airlines.

He encouraged me to keep flying, too. He told me about an airport near where he lived that gave flying lessons. I could complete the training for my private license in a land plane and maybe go on from there to become an instructor. He thought there were positions for female instructors at the flight school and within the FAA.

It was the first time I had heard of a flying position for a woman or been encouraged to pursue it as more than a hobby. It was also the first time I talked with someone from my generation, in the same phase of training, with the same love of flying and similar plans and dreams.

We were far from finishing our conversations when the sun began to rise, first turning the world outside the small oval window pink with the morning light on the clouds below, then too soon filling it with warm golden rays. The morning sun gets bright so much more quickly when you are heading into it at five hundred knots, we agreed, delighting in the shared knowledge of our aviation world.

It was time for me to return to my duties. As I rose from the seat, I wished Sam a fun weekend in London, mentioning that

I had a quick turnaround—I'd be working the return flight the next morning.

Serving breakfast to the cockpit, I heard complaints about not seeing much of me all night. With Sam back in his seat and me checking on passengers, we reverted to our respective roles of customer and employee. Although there was nothing to be embarrassed or ashamed about, I felt I had broken some rule. I knew many flight attendants who openly flirted with passengers, hoping to find Mr. Right or at least a companion for the layover. There was no official rule against it, but that wasn't me, and I didn't want anyone to think that was the situation now.

Sam, whom I had only known for a few hours, now knew the latest version of me better than anyone in my life, and I was pretty sure the situation was mutual. With all of that running through my head and heart, it was a challenge to treat him like any other passenger as I prepared the cabin for landing. I didn't dare look in his direction while I made the necessary pre-arrival announcements.

As he was deplaning with Tom again at his side, I offered a quick "bye," "thank you," and "good luck," the same comments robotically made to all the other passengers who traveled with us. I thought I saw Sam start to turn back as he walked toward the terminal and realized we hadn't exchanged phone numbers. Then he was gone, and I had no way of finding him again.

I spent the layover in my usual routine of walking around London, mixing sightseeing with shopping, and later I joined the rest of the crew for an early dinner. The whole time, my mind kept returning to Sam and our conversation. What if my flying didn't have to stop with the Cub? What if I could pursue this love further? What if we met again?

It was one of those nights all too familiar to international flight crews that finds one suddenly wide awake in a pitch-black room in a hotel struggling to figure out where you are and how you got there, which time zone you're in, and what the clock's red numbers mean: a.m. or p.m.? Had I been asleep for only an hour, and it was going to be a very long night, or had I slept through the wake-up call and the crew was waiting on the bus? Of course, when I finally did fall into a deep sleep, the phone rang to tell me it was time to rise and shine. Rise, maybe. Shine was another matter.

On the plane, after performing our routine safety inspections, my coworker, Laura, agreed to be the greeter so I could hide in the galley. There, I was able to yawn undisturbed, drink coffee like medicine, and check the catering and liquor deliveries. Suddenly my solitude was broken when Laura's head popped between the curtains.

"Hey. They're here again."

"What? Who?"

I closed the oven door, losing count of the lamb chops inside.

"You know, those two cute guys from our flight here."

I poked my head around the corner to see them settling into their same seats with the same confident, home-away-from-home attitude. Had it been only yesterday? Pouring glasses of orange juice, I hoped my excuse to see him didn't appear too lame or forward. I delivered the unrequested beverages with a napkin and a grin.

"I wasn't expecting you guys," I said, trying to sound casual. "I thought you were staying for the weekend."

"So did I," replied Tom, in a less than pleased tone, while glaring at his companion.

"What happened?" I asked, looking from one to the other.

"You," Tom responded again, punching his pillow into the window space.

Sam shrugged and smiled, his blue eyes meeting mine.

8

Next Stop: Miami

The flight home was as awful as the one going to London had been lovely. Finding out that Sam was on board was the only good thing about it. In sharp contrast to the pleasant, calm evening crossing, this time we were leaving in the early afternoon, following the sun as it also moved west, so the flight was entirely in the daylight. During the preflight briefing, the captain warned us of storms over the Atlantic. Storms create turbulence, which in turn create a plane full of unhappy, uncomfortable, airsick passengers confined to their seats; cranky, crying children; and a tense work environment. With one of the flight attendants also ill, I agreed to help in the coach cabin after boarding was complete.

The plane was filled to near capacity, the hungover purser was making Bloody Marys in the back galley, and a passenger was refusing to keep his yippy lapdog in its kennel. A woman dressed, evidently, in nothing but turquoise jewelry and a mink coat, stopped by the galley to hand me clothes she had removed in the lav. She asked that I hang them up, so they would remain unwrinkled while she slept. She then proceeded to her seat, where she used her coat as a blanket. I could only hope that she didn't toss and turn in her sleep.

With all the chaos, Sam soon realized that we would have little opportunity to talk. Walking by me on his way to the lavatory, he slipped a cocktail napkin note into my hand that wished me luck with all the crazies. After that, we resorted to writing to each other like junior high kids between classes. It turned into a fun game and made the otherwise very long day and hectic flight bearable. It also allowed us finally to exchange contact information. Via napkin notes, we concluded that it would be easier for me to go to Miami than for him to come to New York, so I agreed to try to make it happen. I just wasn't sure how. I wasn't senior enough to hold Miami layovers, I couldn't afford a hotel, and I didn't feel comfortable staying with someone I had just met on an airplane.

A few weeks after that flight, my former roommate from Long Beach, Donna, called to catch up. After we worked together on the sailboat in Antigua, she transferred to Delta's Miami base. She asked if I would want to visit anytime. Did I?!?! I wondered if the universe ever tired of my silent thank you for all it laid in my path. I explained about meeting Sam and found out his apartment was near hers on Kendall Avenue.

Soon after I arrived in Miami, Donna was called out for a multi-day flight, and I found time to spend with Sam. Our first stop was Carib Aviation, where Sam took lessons at New Tamiami Airport, on the edge of the Everglades. Carib was an FBO (fixed base operation), an establishment where airplane owners could rent a tie-down space with the option of renting their aircraft to others. It was also where a prospective student could rent a plane and find an instructor.

I had already logged over sixty hours of instruction from flying the Cub, and Dawn had done a good job preparing me for the written exam. I discovered that I could complete the flying and exams required to get my Private Pilot Certificate in two weeks for one thousand dollars. Sam seemed happy at the prospect of my returning to Miami to continue flying and seeing each other. Even Tom said he wouldn't mind if I wanted to hang out at their place. I promised to be back.

It took a few months to save the money from my paychecks and arrange for the time off from TWA. In February 1975, I returned to Miami and flew every day. With the help of my new instructor and Sam, I soon became familiar with the training plane, a Cessna-150. I learned to take off and land on a cement runway and with a crosswind, fly in a traffic pattern, talk on the radio, and use radio navigation. I mastered stall and spin recovery and landing with flaps on short and soft fields. I also completed the required solo cross-country flights.

My two weeks of lessons and all that I had learned flying the Cub in Vermont prepared me well to pass the FAA private pilot written and flight exams. After my successful check ride, the instructors at the FBO congratulated me and encouraged me to continue flying.

The next step would be an instrument rating, which would allow me to fly in low-visibility weather and through clouds. That meant yet another written exam, more flying lessons, another one hundred hours of flight time—and lots more money. It seemed an impossible goal, and part of me wondered why bother, but I was hooked. It was the most interesting, exciting thing I had ever done, and I loved the world it allowed me to enter. I was enjoying the journey, so wherever it took me or ended would be well worth whatever it took to get there.

When he wasn't in class, Sam and I spent time together discovering all the things we had in common. We jogged and rode bikes all over the neighborhood, played tennis, outdoor racquetball, Frisbee, and backgammon. We cooked together, swam, and went to the beach. Our best times were spent flying together, taking turns at the controls and pretending to be instructors for each other. Sam seemed as knowledgeable and capable as anyone at the FBO, even though he was still working on his advanced ratings as well. He never tired of answering questions or demonstrating to help me understand. And he made it fun.

One day he had an airplane engine in pieces on the patio floor, and he invited me to help put it back together. Another day, I helped gap spark plugs in his beloved VW Beetle and learned how to use a timing gun. I had no words to express how endearing I found those simple gestures of help and acceptance into his world or how remarkable it was that he treated me as an equal.

I remembered when I was a little girl watching my dad work with tools that hung in perfect order over the workbench in the farm's machinery shed. The tools seemed like magic wands and keys that could make dead or ailing machines well again. I asked if I would use them, too, someday. Lovingly, he said, "Don't think so, Princess." I had been denied access to that world for some inexplicable reason that I had to accept—until now.

Here, Sam handed me those same tools and more, and I learned that it wasn't magic but knowledge that would open the doors. I was madly in love with flying and this wonderful young man who had so willingly opened his world and his heart to me.

9

Charters

I found balancing my two worlds as a small plane pilot and as an airline flight attendant suited my personality well and caused me to better enjoy both roles. I liked being "one of the guys" at the Miami FBO, dressed in clothes appropriate for climbing in, out, and around airplanes in the heat. However, I also enjoyed donning the classic uniform and looking the part of an international flight attendant to enter the world of first-class travelers.

I liked my job at TWA and worked hard to ensure my passengers had a safe and enjoyable experience. I warmed baby bottles, walked babies, entertained children so parents could sleep, and took care of pets. I kept meals warm for those who weren't hungry but would be later, brought extra servings to those still hungry, and reseated people to make them happy. I was also able to explain the plane's movements and noises to visibly fearful fliers. TWA received letters and cards complimenting me and thanking me for my attention to their needs.

I occasionally got to work special charters on B-707s configured with all-first-class seating—two seats on each side of the aisle and extra legroom. They transported athletic teams, musical groups, and gamblers bound for Las Vegas (LAS). The sports teams and musical groups usually gave us tickets to their events, and the gamblers tipped us money for the casino, a practice unheard of today. In the mid-seventies, a twenty-dollar tip gave me an evening of fun at the two-dollar blackjack table and included dinner. The rumor was that the casinos paid the first-class airfare for these high rollers to come take their chances in "Lost Wages." On the way there, everyone was in a party mood, laughing, drinking, and playing cards. The return flights tended to be a bit more somber.

On one LAS flight, a first-class passenger who owned hotels and casinos on the Strip traveled with a new puppy he had just purchased in New York. The poor thing was whining in his carrier under the seat, so after takeoff, I offered to help. I lined the area around my jump seat with papers and a blanket so it could move around. The female cabin crew took turns petting and holding the little cutie that soon fell asleep on the blanket. My passenger rewarded me with a one-hundred-dollar tip I shared with my co-workers. He invited all of us to his house for a party, sending a limo to transport us to his mansion. It was fascinating to see that lifestyle in person—until the scene became uncomfortable with drugs, alcohol, and an offer to "find a partner" for extra pay. I was surprised to learn some girls who regularly worked the charters supplemented their income this way. The limo driver kindly complied with my request to return to the hotel.

On another LAS layover, one of the other flight attendants and I walked down the Strip deciding which casino would get our money. We had no illusions of taking any of it home and knew to stop when it was gone. Las Vegas was a make-believe city of flashing lights and Monopoly money where nothing seemed real or solid, and I loved it in one-night doses.

I can't remember which casino we chose. When my luck and money ran out, I looked around for my friend and found her at the side of a roulette wheel player who considered her his latest Lady Luck. Waving me on, she indicated that she was fine with my returning to the hotel without her. I headed for the enormous revolving door at the corner entrance.

A handsome young man in his twenties held open the side door and smiled a "good evening." I assumed that was his job until he stepped out right behind me and started talking.

"Nice evening, isn't it?"

I looked over at him with surprise and took in my surroundings. Although it was close to midnight, the street was as bright and full of people as if it were midday. It seemed safe enough to talk to a handsome stranger in a place where weird was normal.

"Why, yes, it is," I responded, smiling.

"On your way to the Western?" he asked.

That stopped me in my tracks. The Western Hotel was where airline crews generally stayed on layovers, but how could he know I was staying there? It felt invasive. He seemed nice enough, but…

"Yeah, my family is staying there," I lied. "They went on ahead and are waiting for me."

I looked away and picked up the pace. I'm a terrible liar, but knowing how some flight attendants spent their overnights, I didn't want to admit to being one to him.

In a gentlemanly gesture, he moved to walk on the street side of the sidewalk.

"I'm going that way," he said. "Mind if I walk with you?"

I couldn't help but grin and let down my guard a bit. What deviant would want to follow an outdated custom protecting a lady from being splashed by water in the street?

"Your mother teach you that?"

"Yep. She insisted on raising a gentleman."

Seeing me relax, he explained that he had just gotten off work at the casino we left and thought offering to walk with me would be a kind gesture. I agreed that it was and allowed him to choose a shortcut he knew. As we walked, he talked about his family, his life, the city—or rather, he performed it. He had me laughing out loud as I followed along.

"Hey, let's duck into the Sahara," he said, suddenly taking my hand and turning a corner to a side entrance of the big casino. The door opened into an enormous, brightly lit kitchen with cooks and waiters running around frantically. They each stopped for just a second to say, "Hi, Sandy," "Hey, Sandy," "Lookin' good, Sandy," as they nodded at me and smiled. I realized we hadn't exchanged names, and his hand in mine felt nice. Evidently, he was Sandy, and this wasn't the first time he had entered through the kitchen. I thought maybe he worked there, too.

Sandy tugged me along through another door that opened into a large room lit only with candles. When my eyes adjusted from the bright kitchen fluorescents to the candlelight, I saw a room filled with people sitting around small circular tables topped with black tablecloths and red glass globes with candles. On the stage to my left, a man had the entire audience in laughter. Sandy spotted an empty table for two right in front. Pulling me toward it, and ever the gentleman, he pulled the chair out for me to sit before sitting down himself like he owned the place.

Immediately, a waiter appeared with a Coke for Sandy and asked what I wanted. I just shook my head. I knew enough to know that these dinner clubs and shows were expensive and required reservations. I could not fathom what had just happened, and I didn't want to be part of a joke or in trouble. I tapped Sandy on the arm to ask for an explanation, but he just motioned to be quiet so that he could hear the performance.

We were watching Buddy Hackett, a big-name nightclub comedian, and he was hilarious. The routine was a bit crude at times, for which he was famous, but within limits. The audience loved him, and I could see why. He was adorable, an R-rated version of the Pillsbury doughboy. As he was finishing his set, he turned toward our table.

"It looks like my son joined us tonight. Sandy, say Hello."

The guy at my table started to stand up as a spotlight came across the crowd toward us. I was mortified. Just because his name was also Sandy, I thought, he should not take the prank that far. I pulled on his shirt to make him sit back down. He took my hand to stop me and whispered, "It's okay. It's me." He waved to the room as everyone applauded, and I tried to disappear into my chair. Buddy finished his show to loud applause as the curtains drew closed.

"We can go now if you want," Sandy said quietly, trying to judge my mood. I was in shock and couldn't register a response. "Or we could go backstage. Want to meet Buddy?"

"You mean '*Dad*'?" I asked in a controlled voice. The house lights had come on. The stage show was over, but the one at our table had just begun. I was still feeling mortified. How had I looked to that room full of people while trying to make him sit down?

"Why didn't you tell me we were going to see your dad perform – and that you—*we*—would be in a spotlight?"

He was ready with his comeback, "Why didn't you admit to being a flight attendant?"

That caught me off guard.

"What? How did you know?"

"All the flight crews stay at the Western. I saw you with your friend – definitely not your sister. Besides, you look and act like a flight attendant on a layover using your tip money."

"I'm not sure that's a compliment. Okay, I guess I deserve revenge deceit."

The comedy of the whole thing was starting to sink in.

"Sure. I'd love to meet your dad," I said, able to smile again.

We went backstage where Buddy Hackett was chatting with folks and still making them laugh as if it were just his natural way. He stopped to meet me and talk with Sandy. The father-son relationship was obviously one of love and mutual respect. My main thought in seeing them together, however, was that Buddy's wife must be a very tall, beautiful woman who gave Sandy her genes. I'm sure Buddy would be the first to agree.

Now that we knew the truth about each other, we could relax and be honest. We talked for hours, walking up and down the Strip. Sandy hoped to follow in his father's footsteps, make it as a stand-up comedian, and champion other people who wanted to make it to the big time. We stayed in touch, remained friends, and got together when we could. Sandy did succeed in fulfilling his dream as a team with his wife.

I have very few regrets in my life. However, I regret declining Sandy's invitation to a Halloween party in Los Angeles hosted by Johnny Carson. I was nervous about meeting famous people, concerned about a costume, and I couldn't get the time off. I couldn't call in sick and then get on a flight to LA. Not figuring out how to make it to that party will haunt me forever. On television one night, I watched Johnny talking with one of his guests about what a fabulous time everyone had at his party – without me.

One other memorable charter was for a historic event. I was part of the crew on the plane that followed Air Force One taking President Ford to Paris in November 1975 for an economic summit with other world leaders. Our 707 waited on the ground while the president and his detail boarded Air Force One and took off. The press corps took pictures, got responses to their questions, and filmed Air Force One's departure before scrambling to their seats and typewriters on our plane. They were frantic to put their notes into a story for their publications. I cannot remember how or whether they transmitted their stories to their papers while airborne.

The scene on that plane was unlike anything I had ever experienced. All the rules were out the window, and protocols were ignored. Cigarette smoke and an excited tension filled the air. The stress had everything to do with getting a news story filed before a deadline and nothing to do with being on a plane. These were seasoned travelers.

Departure announcements and safety demonstrations were drowned out by the sound of a hundred typewriters clacking away and ignored by men deep in thought and busy writing. During takeoff, tray tables were down, covered with typewriters, clipboards, and notebooks. Seatbelts seemed to be optional. I have no idea how we would have accomplished an emergency evacuation. The cockpit door remained open during the entire flight. The specially selected pilots who flew these charters explained the new rules—or lack thereof—to me since I was the new kid on the block.

Our passengers did *not* want to be served or bothered. Instead of individual meals that would have taken up space on the tray table and required the passenger to stop working, the meal service consisted of large trays of cold cuts, cheeses, bread and rolls, and a fruit platter laid out in the galleys for the guys to get when they wished. I noticed no female reporters and wondered whether there were none, like no female pilots. We took the beverage carts with liquor, beer, coffee, and water up and down the aisle every ten minutes. The makings for ice cream sundae desserts sat out until all were eaten. For those who wanted to sleep, we dimmed the lights and handed out the pillows and blankets. A few of the men continued working with their overhead lamps on. They would all have to get back to work immediately after landing in Paris. We had pastries and coffee ready when they awoke.

Our flight time was much shorter than usual. Our 707 had to fly faster, overtake Air Force One, and land first. Fuel efficiency was not a factor. The reporters needed to deplane and be in position to film the president's arrival and official greeting. After more filming, photos, and interviews, the reporters gathered their suitcases and typewriters and boarded a bus waiting for us. I was surprised to find the bus was also for the airline crew—no crew hotel this time.

The airline had booked our rooms at the same hotel as the newsmen—the George V, a five-star luxury Parisian hotel where we would stay for the week. The news crews covered the summit, sent in their reports during the day, and enjoyed the Paris nightlife in the evenings. The crew was invited along as the French played hostess to their American guests.

The French are charming hosts. Every evening included an exquisite meal and a cabaret show, the most memorable of which was the famous *Moulin Rouge*. During the pre-show dinner, it seemed each diner had their own, white-gloved waiter serving and removing course after course of delicious food, creatively presented. I still remember the special dessert was gender-specific with innuendo that only the French can pull off. The men got two scoops of vanilla ice cream with cherries atop each mound. For the women, a banana protruded between the cold white ice cream balls. Toppings were available to customize the delicacy.

The show was also something I will never forget. Beautiful women with more material in their elaborate headpieces than on their identical well-endowed bodies moved in choreographed, high-kicking precise routines. It was incredible, but that was just the opener. A room-sized aquarium appeared on stage filled with beautiful mermaids performing a synchronized underwater routine. I have no idea how those women held their breath so long while exerting such energy yet looking completely controlled and relaxed. I wasn't over that amazing scene when the curtain rose again. A horse ran at full gallop to the very end of the stage, where it suddenly stopped to rear up on its hind legs! It was the opening to a Western-themed cabaret revue. I had never seen anything so daring or beautiful. At age twenty-four, I burned it into my memory as one of the most fantastic entertainment experiences of my life.

I framed my souvenir matchbook from Air Force One as a reminder that it was all real.

1974

10

Gulls and Girls in Madrid

Because flights to European cities took too long to do a turn-around (return to New York the same day), flight crews had almost twenty-four hours to enjoy our destinations. My favorite city for a layover was Madrid. I enjoyed the city, the people, and practicing Spanish. We flight crews became friends with our Spanish gate agents who often joined us for dinner and showed us the night life at the local tapas or bars. Over dinner one evening, I mentioned that I would love to improve my high school Spanish and get a true taste of the culture by living and working in Madrid someday. They explained that many young Americans found jobs as English teachers at night schools for businesspeople. When they heard that I had a degree and experience as an English teacher, they agreed that I would be in high demand. They enthusiastically offered to help me find a job with a good salary and comfortable schedule. However, they were unable to help with suggestions for housing. Young people there lived with their parents until they married, and then the newly-weds moved in with one set of their parents until the first child was due. Finding a single roommate or an apartment for one person would be impossible, so I shelved the idea.

On the flight back home, while I was studying and chatting with the guys in the cockpit, I mentioned my wish to live and work in Madrid someday. The captain said that idea worked perfectly for him. He kept an apartment there to keep from paying US taxes. It needed to appear to be occupied a few months each year. I could have free use of it if I paid the utilities and picked up the mail. It was too perfect of an opportunity to pass up. I had learned when the Universe hands you what you just asked for, you better say "Yes" if you want it to keep happening.

We made a handshake deal, and everything fell into place. On the next layover my Spanish friends helped me find a job at the language school Centro Britanico, whose students were mainly bankers wanting to serve international clients. With my degree in English Ed, the school administrator was excited to hire me and would pay more than my TWA salary. However, there was one requirement. I needed to speak and teach proper British English. They didn't want the students learning "gutter" American English.

No problem. I had flown London often enough to know how to adopt the accent, especially after a few days of hearing it from the other truly British teachers. I knew lift, lorry, boot, zed, telly and the expression no American could say without a snicker— "knock you up," meaning to stop by to visit. It was agreed that I would work the afternoon shift from two o'clock to eight o'clock. That left the mornings for studying for my instrument and commercial written exams.

My leave of absence request from TWA was approved for three months and I moved into the small apartment on Avenido Generalisimo. After receiving strange looks when I boarded the bus at my corner, I discovered I was living in the red-light district in a country where only "working girls" lived alone. The captain had failed to mention this important detail.

I made friends with the other instructors and enjoyed my days off getting to know the city's beautiful sights and rich history. Weekends were spent with my new friends from school taking trips to the coastal towns. Each morning, I took my coffee and books across the street to a park to study. I tried to be disciplined about it so that I could pass the written exams upon my return to the States.

Getting to actually live in a foreign country rather than rushing through the tourist highlights in a 24-hour snapshot visit during a layover was so much more enjoyable. I fell into routines that blended experiencing my new world while staying connected to the old. I loved the daily trips to the market where everything was purchased fresh. With limited refrigeration, it was a necessary chore I looked forward to each morning. Colorful arrays of fresh fruit and vegetables lay next to raw meat hung from hooks, still-feathered chickens hung by their feet, and whole fish lay on wooden counters. The wine store filled the jug I brought along from a huge vat. The bread was baked fresh each day. My street Spanish improved out of necessity.

The language school closed over the Easter holiday week, so I made plans for a quick trip home. I asked what my coworkers would like me to bring them from the States. My female friends wanted chocolate. The males asked for copies of Playboy and condoms, neither of which I had ever purchased before. It did not occur to me to ask why they didn't get those things themselves, nor did I realize both were illegal in Franco's Spain of 1973.

Back in New York, I went to the local drugstore, thinking I could do one-stop shopping. I found the large Hershey bars on sale for the girls and back issues of Playboy for the guys. Then I went to the pharmacy counter to fulfill the last item on the list, trying to act casual.

"I'd like a large box of condoms, please."

"You would? What brand?"

I had a feeling my flustered expression and inability to make eye contact gave me away. The middle-aged clerk behind the counter was smiling too much.

"Uh—Oh, whatever you think is the usual one, I guess."

"Well, what size? There's a nice variety of materials, textures, colors and even scents and tastes. What's your favorite?"

Having had no experience in this area, I tried the line I used when confronted with too many choices. "Oh, just give me a few of each."

"This isn't a donut shop," he said almost laughing out loud now, "but I can give you an assorted dozen."

He lay a variety of twelve down on the counter for my approval and started to put them in a small box beside the chocolate bars and magazines. He was having a great time with my obvious discomfort—which got worse as I thought of all the guys who had put in a request.

"Oh, I'm going to need a whole lot more than that," I blurted out.

"You are?" He looked up to see if I was now the one having too much fun.

I was not. I could feel myself turning red as I tried to explain.

"Well, I just thought there would be more than that in a box. There's a lot of them—guys I mean. And I don't want them disappointed." This just kept getting worse.

The guy could hardly contain himself. "I'm sure you don't."

I wanted him to understand and stop smirking.

"Look, they're for work. I mean, for the guys at work."

"Yes, it usually is for the guys—at your 'work'."

The way he said it made it sound awful. I just wanted to disappear.

The clerk was waiting for me to share more information that would make his previously dull day even better. I was afraid to open my mouth. I just stood there, staring at the small box that had caused so much trouble, wanting the whole ordeal to be over.

Breaking the uncomfortable silence, he retrieved a box that had three of the smaller boxes inside and plopped it down on the counter.

"So, a larger box—like this? Do you think this will be enough for all your guys?"

"Sure," I said, wanting the nightmare to end.

"Do you still want me to mix them up for you—all different sizes and types?"

"Yes, please," I said quietly, still unable to meet his eyes.

I couldn't believe how expensive it was, but there was no way I was going to argue or change anything. I couldn't wait to grab the bag with the troublesome box inside and rush to the door. I almost made it outside to safety when the man called out for everyone to hear, "Uh, miss, lady with the condoms, you forgot your candy and Playboys."

The trip to the drugstore to fulfill the wish lists left the store owner laughing and me mortified, but it was nothing compared to the scene that could have occurred going through Spanish customs. Because I packed the gifts with my clothes in my flight attendant luggage and went through customs with the crew, no one checked the contents. I only found out later that I had arrived with a suitcase full of contraband and could have been put in jail. Playboy magazines were considered pornography, and condoms were birth-control. Both were illegal in 1973 in Franco's Catholic Spain. Smuggling in items wasn't looked on kindly.

In addition to the gifts for my friends, I returned to Madrid with gifts for myself — books by my favorite author Richard Bach. I had always loved to read and found it a good way to spend the quiet hours alone in the apartment or relaxing in the park. After hours of studying facts and figures for the instrument and commercial exams, I escaped into the world of fiction and fantasy. Even there, however, I was drawn to flying.

I began reading Bach's books in the early 70's as I was taking my first flying lessons. In his best-seller, *Jonathan Livingston Seagull* (Scribner 1970), it seemed Jonathan was talking to me. In the little Cub on Lake Champlain, I, too, flew over the water. I could have been on the beach when he spoke to his flock of gulls.

"It is right for a gull (I read 'girl') to fly. That freedom is the very nature of his (her) being, that whatever stands against that freedom must be set aside." Just as Johnathan was told, "Gulls can't fly high or fast," I was told, "Girls can't fly as commercial airplane pilots."

In *Illusions*, I read, "You are never given a wish without also being given the power to make it true. You may have to work for it, however," and I'd hit the books more determined than ever. I read Bach's books one after the other: *Nothing by Chance, Stranger to the Ground, A Gift of Wings,* using them as inspiration and a well-deserved break after hours of study.

Before I left for Madrid, I had the opportunity to take both of my grandfathers on their first and only plane ride over their Southern Illinois farms. It was a perfect sunlit day that I held in my heart, thinking it could never be put into words. Bach's books, however, brought back those sweet memories in such detail it was hard to believe he hadn't been there, too. In *Biplane*, his description of flying over the Midwest perfectly captured the view of crops growing in fields, farmers working the land; the movements and sensations of flight; the sheer beauty seen from aloft. My feelings and thoughts were on his pages. Remembering my grandpas' reaction of leaning away from the window as I banked to give them a better look made me smile. We finished the flight straight and level. They didn't say a word during the flight but had lots to tell their friends.

Bach's writings continued to motivate and speak to me. "How much more there is now to living! We can find ourselves as creatures of excellence and intelligence and skill. We can be free! We can learn to fly!"

It wasn't just the view of a rural landscape that Bach seemed to have lifted from my soul, but also his view of the spiritual world. Here again, he put part of me, my nascent spiritual beliefs, into words better than I had even thought them in my head. His writing was my first introduction to metaphysics and New Age thought, although it would be many years before I would hear those terms. Just as his description of flying captured the very essence of flight, so did his characters and their stories capture the essence of the Laws of the Universe, Cosmic Cause and Effect. His characters believed there were no accidents, that we create our own reality in a universe where we are an integral part of All. I found myself nodding at the pages thinking, *Yes, yes, that's it exactly!*

Finally, I felt I had to tell Mr. Bach directly, so I sat down to write my first and only fan letter. I tried to express how his writing had touched me, how I envied his experiences and adventures, touching Nature and lives, finding his heart's purpose, the meaning to Life and Love in the cockpit of a plane. I shared with him my dream to be a pilot, too, and my plans to make it come true. I told him I was a private pilot working hard on my instrument and commercial ratings but didn't know how it was going to work out.

I was astonished when he responded with a note instructing me to open an account titled "Airplane Fund." to put all my birthday and Christmas monetary gifts into it to be used for flying lessons, and to know that all I hoped for would happen. I was even more stunned to find he had included a check for one hundred dollars with his encouraging note. Soon, he assured me, there would be the means to take the next step and the next and the next.

After I returned to Florida, Richard Bach flew his plane from his home in Winter Haven to Tamiami Airport where I got to meet and thank him in person. Years later (1986) Richard introduced me on a BBC special called "Reaching for the Skies" where we were both featured. It can be viewed on YouTube today by going to YouTube/Reaching for the Skies and select Episode 2.

Teaching in Madrid

Grandpas' first flight

11

One Expensive Hobby

I did as Bach instructed and opened "Lynn's Flying Fund" with his hundred-dollar check. To add to it, I worked more, saved more, and directed all gifts to my flying account. However, the traditional crisp two-dollar bill inside my birthday card from grandparents, even the more generous twenty dollars from godparents and parents, did little more than make the journey look further away and steeper. As I placed a lovely twenty-three-dollar blouse back on the store rack, I reminded myself that it was one hour of flying hanging there. The "stuff vs. flight time" argument was becoming a common theme.

"That's one expensive hobby you got goin' there," My father said, voicing what I'm sure most were thinking, adding, "I sure hope you find someone rich to marry."

I couldn't argue with the first part of his statement, but I had decided early on that I would rather live on whatever income I could make happily doing what I loved rather than trying to earn enough to be happy. I also swore I would never depend on a man or anyone else for my happiness. I knew I could never have a career or make a living as a pilot, but my flight attendant salary paid for my habit and my simple lifestyle, so I felt I needed no more. My biggest fear of ever being bored was certainly put to rest, and the desire to continue learning was met.

I took the written exams for the instrument rating and commercial pilot certificate and passed with flying colors (pun intended). However, I also needed the flight time and lessons required to take the accompanying FAA flight check rides. I was short over one hundred hours for the instrument, almost two hundred for the commercial. However, I did have enough hours to return to Vermont for my seaplane rating and to thank Dawn and Bill for all they had done.

I split my time between New York to work for TWA and Miami to take flying lessons at Carib Aviation. After several trips to Miami, I began spending more time with Sam than with Donna, and bit by bit, I moved my Miami belongings to his place. Sam's folks owned the condo. Tom and I helped pay for utilities, bought groceries, and I cooked when I was there. I still had a place in New York, my flight attendant base, where I had to pay rent. It was a precarious balance between working enough to make money for lessons and finding time off to take those lessons. I had no idea where any of it would lead, but I was really enjoying the journey. Taking it one step at a time while looking or waiting for solutions to arise seemed to have worked well so far.

A partial solution to the income problem came, thanks to the manager at Carib, where I was taking lessons. While Sam attended classes during the day, I hung out at the airport, helping however I could. Carib's manager hired me to answer phones and be a general gofer, things I was doing anyway.

The instructors also provided some help. They liked teaching the flying lessons because they got to log the flight hours, but no one wanted to teach the ground school information. I found I could take the simple written exam to be a BSI, basic ground school instructor, and qualify to prepare students for their written exams. The course explained how various people learn differently and how to teach each one effectively. I already had a degree in it! Little did I imagine I would use my teaching degree to teach flying! In return for giving their students ground school, the instructors gave me flying lessons.

My favorite ground school class was one I created, advertised, and then taught for pilots' wives and girlfriends. They learned basic airplane lingo, aerodynamics, radio usage, chart reading and navigation, and how to read the plane's instruments. It made accompanying their flight-loving partner more fun—and safer in case their knowledge was ever needed. I enjoyed removing mystique to make it simple and fun for everyone. They seemed to enjoy the class immensely and tipped handsomely.

Although I didn't get paid, I volunteered at local schools for science fairs to teach aerodynamics and Bernoulli's principle of hydrodynamics. I ended the lesson by giving each student a balsa wood model airplane to fly, adjusting the control surfaces of the airfoils to demonstrate the lesson. I loved being in front of a class again. The nearby Hughes helicopter dealership hired me to teach the ground school portion of the flying lessons offered with each helicopter purchase.

My first students were two young brothers from Venezuela who spoke limited English, so we struggled through with my conversational Spanish. I asked their father if he would also be in the class. He had purchased three Hughes 300s, so he had paid for three ground schools.

"*No quiere estar en clase tambien?*" (Don't you want to be in class, too?)

"*No. los helicopteros son por mis hijos.*" (No, the helicopters are for my sons.)

"*Usted tiene dos hijos, pero tres helicopterors. Por que?*" (You have two sons but three helicopters. Why?)

"*Entiendo que chocan con frequencia.*" (I understand they crash a lot.)

How comforting for his sons, I thought.

My Spanish from high school and Madrid wasn't as helpful as I had hoped with the different Venezuelan accent and minimal knowledge of aviation terms. I think I put in more preparation and hard work for that class than any other I taught.

Working with the helicopter students allowed me to meet their flight instructors, who offered helicopter lessons, which I gladly accepted. During one lesson, we spotted a patch of wild strawberries that could only be accessed by dropping in, going straight down as only a helicopter can do. They were the sweetest strawberries I ever tasted, and it was the most fun I ever had picking some. However, my final analysis of helicopter flying was amazement that the inventor of such a contraption had lived, that anyone would get in it more than once, or that it was considered "flying" at all. I joined the group of fixed-wing pilots who jokingly agreed the only reason a helicopter got into the air was that it was so ugly, the ground rejected it.

Another offer for flight instruction I received—and rejected—was for aerobatics. A friend of Sam's flew a Pitts Special for the Budweiser aerobatic team in airshows and was an excellent pilot. However, he was having trouble passing his instrument written exam, which he needed to enjoy regular flying. I agreed to continue teaching him instrument ground school until he received a passing grade in return for time in the Pitts. After a few rides with barrel rolls, inside and outside loops, hammerhead stalls, and tight spins, I decided it was something I would have to do a lot or not at all—and chose the latter.

The mechanics often needed an extra pair of hands to hold the flashlight, hand them a tool, or help with a procedure. I especially liked helping Jim, a Pan Am mechanic, who seemed to live at the airport and worked on his plane way more than he flew it. The plane was an old twin-engine Piper Apache that had no paint. It reflected the Florida sun with a shiny buffed metal exterior. The interior was just as bare. With all the cabin's material removed, I could watch the cables move from the front control column and rudder pedals to the tail and wings' control surfaces. I helped bleed the brake lines or move the controls as he made adjustments. In return, I received precious twin-engine time and lessons.

Sam and I continued to study, practice, and fly together. We shared logging the time we flew over the Everglades for lunch at the Marathon Key airport cafe, to Freeport to visit his parents, to the practice area for spins and stalls, or just staying in the pattern for touch-and-goes. He was learning material in his classes at Miami Dade that I was trying to understand on my own by reading the handbooks and text guides, so he often helped explain things. To practice instrument flying, we took turns playing air traffic controller and pilot in our living room. Holding an invisible yoke, we "flew" to pillows on the floor representing the VOR (very-high-frequency omnidirectional-range receiver) and NDB (non-directional beacon), which were ground-based navigational aids.

"Seneca Four Two Papa, on present heading intercept the one-four-zero radial and fly TO the station to hold on the tree-six-zero degree radial. Right-hand turns."

Or "Seneca Four Two Papa, proceed directly to the NDB and fly the two-seven-zero degree bearing outbound to intercept the VOR one-eight-zero degree radial. Left-hand turns."

As he issued orders into his cupped hand holding a pretend mike, I walked around our small pea-green carpeted living room, leaning left and right, deciding whether the holding pattern entry should be tear-drop or parallel, then going in circles to comply with air traffic controller's order. We practiced in the plane as well, taking turns in the student and teacher roles while flying somewhere for lunch, splitting the check and the precious flight time.

My TWA supervisor in New York, who knew of my other life in Miami, told me about "butterfly leaves" offered to flight attendants. The leaves of absence would allow me to take up to six months off during the slower winter months while maintaining seniority and benefits. Now I could concentrate on my flying in Miami and spend more time with Sam. It seemed the universe was again cooperating, offering solutions to help me reach a goal and to be happy.

From 1973 to 1977, I used butterfly leaves and time off to acquire my commercial license, instrument and multi-engine ratings, and CFI (certificated flight instructor) certificate, and finally the ATP (air transport pilot) license. Over time, I was accepted into the all-male community by the guys who also spent their days working and playing at the small airport, doing what they loved—flying. Best of all, I was finally able to have my expensive hobby pay for itself!

12

Flying and Life Lessons

Flight instructing was the path of choice for most civilian pilots who wanted to earn a bit of money while building the flight time needed for airline applications. After obtaining my certificate, I was immediately hired at Carib Aviation as a CFI (a certificated flight instructor) and joined the group of guys who helped me get there. I had a degree and experience in teaching, so I felt confident in my ability to help my students learn the written material. However, I also had to demonstrate all I was teaching in the plane and have the student follow my example.

Although flight instructing was the lowest paying flight position, I concluded it had to be the most dangerous and that the industry had it backward. The big bucks go to the airline captains flying the largest planes with the most advanced technology. People on the ground and in the air are trained to help them do their job. The planes they fly have double- and triple-system backups if anything should go wrong, and they are always on someone's radar screen. These guys can communicate with teams of experts anytime, anywhere. Their job is to fly as smoothly as possible from point A to B. These pilots sit in comfort and are served drinks and meals while being paid very well.

In contrast, flight instructors fly the most basic planes with minimal instrumentation, outdated technology, and no backups or assistance. Their role is to put the inexperienced student in new and potentially dangerous configurations and situations such as takeoffs and landings in all weather and ground conditions, spins and stalls, engine failures, and every conceivable emergency—and then wait and hope the student applies what has been taught to correct the situation unassisted. The instructor's decision and timing are critical. She can't jump in to help too soon, or the lesson isn't learned, and worse, confidence is eroded instead of built. However, stepping in too late is far worse. All this responsibility is the instructor's, who is paid a minimal wage.

Preparing students for their private pilot certificate requires instruction from the Pilot's Handbook of Aeronautical Knowledge to pass the written exam and a minimum of forty hours of flight training to pass the FAA's flight exam. Most students can solo after ten hours, so the remaining time is a combination of practice with and without an instructor. The time has to include a solo cross country with three fifty-mile legs—or greater—to demonstrate the ability to navigate correctly.

Instruction also includes landing pattern procedures and takeoffs and landings of all types—soft and short field, flap and no flap, and crosswind. Engine failure and emergency procedures are also practiced. Airwork includes maneuvers showing good control of the plane and recovery from stalls and spins. It is essential students feel comfortable with these before their solo, so they can take corrective actions as needed.

Insufficient airflow over the wing causes the plane to "stall" or stop creating the lift that allows it to stay in the air. A spin is a stall that goes into a tight rotation. Recovery from both is simply to lower the nose and add a bit of rudder if needed. However, it's against one's first instinct to point the nose at the ground, the very thing the pilot is trying to avoid.

Planes have two sets of controls, one in front of each pilot in the cockpit. As the instructor, I demonstrated what the student would then attempt to repeat. There was an understanding that when I said, "I've got it," the student would immediately comply by relinquishing the controls. Most students had no problem with the directive. However, there was always the rare exception.

One day a large boy came in with his father, who did all the talking and signed his son up for lessons. He was unpleasantly surprised that a girl would be the instructor. I pointed out the positive side that I was the lightest weight, which would be a plus in training. When the boy seemed to have no interest and was hesitant to take the controls, I assumed he agreed with his dad, so I suggested a different instructor. He confided that he hadn't wanted the lessons and would never fly solo, but he wanted to keep coming to please his father. He also wanted me to continue as his instructor. Over time, he began enjoying the more basic lessons.

Feeling obligated to try to cover the material, I demonstrated a stall, instructing him to hold the yoke in front of him to better feel the maneuver. When it came time to recover by releasing the back pressure to let the nose drop, he froze stiff-armed, pulling the nose higher in a vain attempt to get away from the ground. My "I've got it," yelled over the sound of the shaking plane, caused no response. He stared straight ahead and kept pulling. I finally yelled "Hey!" and punched his arm as hard as I could. Fortunately, it got his attention, he snapped out of it, and I recovered safely. We were both pretty shaken. I suggested we cut the lesson short and discuss what happened on the ground over a Coke, my treat. He happily agreed.

I didn't think the incident had affected me that much until my nightmare that night. I relived the scene with much more fear than I remembered feeling. In my dream, the kid didn't let go until I delivered a karate chop to his neck. The dream version had us much closer to the ground and about to crash before recovering. I awoke in a sweat and panic, but with a new plan should the situation occur again.

I also decided the boy and I would have to find a way to explain to his father that flying wasn't for everyone and that the young man should be allowed to find some activity of his choosing. It was clear that fear and flying did not mix well. Ironically, the fear of dying could kill you.

During the time I was instructing, the FAA wisely decided to stop requiring spin recovery training since it caused more accidents and deaths than it prevented. The solution was worse than the problem.

In addition to freezing at the controls, there were plenty of other ways students could attempt to ruin the day. They could stomp on the wrong rudder in spin recovery or confuse communication and navigation radio tuning heads during flight. When landing, they might flare or stop the descent too late, early, high, or low. Each time I thought I had seen and heard it all, there would be another "Wait 'til you hear this one" story.

The Florida heat didn't help. There was little air circulation in the Cessna 150 trainer, and the bright sun beat down through the windscreen. After an hour of stalls and spins, I sometimes needed the student to chock and tie down the plane while I went behind the hangar to throw up.

Another flight school that used the same airport had a contract to train Venezuelan students to be commercial pilots for their national airline. The young men received monetary rewards and gold watches for successfully passing each milestone along the way. After returning home, they would train to be jet airline pilots. However, they had so many problems in initial training and had damaged and crashed so many planes when flying solo that they were prohibited from flying alone. A special ruling allowed them to "solo" with the instructor and count the time as PIC (pilot in command) if the instructor didn't touch the controls. Their call sign was always prefaced with "Papa Tango," (pilot trainee). While practicing around the airport, if we heard "Papa Tango coming in," we scattered until PT was safely on the ground.

I had always enjoyed teaching, so my time as a flight instructor is full of fond memories. I loved seeing how learning to fly enriched my students' lives, even their personalities. My favorite moment was greeting my students when they emerged from the plane after soloing with "I DID IT!" in their eyes and smiles. One young, generally shy, slightly awkward seventeen-year-old girl yelled across the ramp for her dad and all to hear, "That was ME!" while pointing to the sky.

It was a special moment at the end of the course when the FAA validated all the student's hard work and study with a private pilot certificate. The small piece of paper said to the world, "I can handle IT—whatever IT is—with no fear." Outwardly, my students left the flight school and me looking the same—but forever changed in how they saw the world and themselves.

13
Coffee Shop Stories

During my six-month leaves of absence, Sam welcomed me back to the apartment on Kendall Drive, which had become our home. I continued taking and giving flying lessons at Tamiami airport, just a few miles down the road. The other instructors, who also spent their days working and flying there, were brothers-in-arms. Like me, they had the strong desire to go beyond just the private pilot level. They studied, flew, and took tests and check rides to obtain their instrument and multi-engine ratings and commercial and instructor certificates. Finally, we were paid for what we loved to do.

Gradually, I was accepted into their community and invited to join my male peers at the TAC-Air Coffee Shop, the gathering place and setting for the telling of tales. Some were legend and lore that may have had some truth at one point but grew over the years with each telling. Other stories had eyewitnesses to swear to their accuracy. Flying, an activity that combined the everchanging elements of weather, machinery, and human nature, was sure to regularly include an unexpected event. Each adventure included examples of testing knowledge and character, providing a new experience for the pilot and another story for the group. Anecdotes were handed down from those who came before and had moved on to better jobs. The pilots were gone, but the yarns lived on. Perhaps some learning took place from hearing others' decisions and the outcomes, but mostly we were there just to talk flying.

In addition to our students' stories, we shared weather and mechanical problems. Forced landings in unintended places like plowed fields, country roads, and horse pastures made great saved-by-the-skin-of-my-teeth anecdotes. We illustrated the accounts on a red checkered tablecloth—a plastic knife served as the runway or road, the napkin dispenser as the stand of trees at its end, and the fork and spoon held in opposite hands were the airplanes demonstrating the latest close calls that required quick thinking and nerves of steel.

Watching my fellow pilots talk with hands and utensils "flying," I recalled a similar scene from childhood. My grandmother's dining room table was where my father, grandfather, uncle, great-uncle, cousins, and hired hands gathered at noon for dinner on the farm. Coming in from the fields, they talked, teased, and laughed over platters of fried meat, potatoes, overcooked vegetables, and warm rhubarb custard pie my grandmother made before the sun came up. I enjoyed listening to their stories and jokes, envying their easy camaraderie. I hoped I would join them someday—until I was old enough to realize entering their men-only world would never happen. They, too, lived their profession. They loved and needed the land the way my pilot peers loved and needed the sky. I hoped that this time, maybe, I could be included in the close-knit group.

As struggling pilots hungry for flight hours, pay, and experience, we accepted whatever job was offered by just about anyone. It could be from businesses with interdepartmental mail to transfer, banks moving canceled checks, ranchers wanting to view their property from the air, real estate agents selling large acreage, gamblers going to Freeport or Nassau, or family members retrieving bodies of loved ones.

The Bermuda Triangle, between Florida and the Bahamas, is a popular setting for stories of unexplained events, disappearances, and haunted planes. Someone always had the latest dead-body-in-a-black-bag story about a corpse that moaned, groaned, sang, spoke, and even sat upright during flight. Aspects of the tales could be true because air inside the body escapes, flowing over the vocal cords as the airplane climbs; involuntary muscle movements or a bit of turbulence can cause the body to shift during flight. However, embellishment seemed mandatory.

A favorite story was about a pilot who was tired of being treated poorly by a demanding, rich client vacationing on an exclusive island off the Florida coast. The final straw came when she needed him to fly her to Boston so her cat could go to its favorite vet. The lady handed the pilot her luggage, fur coat, and empty pet carrier to put in the cargo hold. She planned to use the carrier only after they landed. He explained that the cat had to be in the carrier during the flight and refused to take off until she complied. The spoiled puss was finally put into its travel container for take-off, but the lady let it out to sit on her lap the moment they left the runway. The terrified animal started running circles inside the cabin, meowing loudly while the pilot was trying to fly and hear departure instructions on the radio. The cat was screeching and scampering laps across the back of the pilot's seat, jumping up on the dashboard, and trying to get outside. As it came by again, clawing over his head and shoulders, he nonchalantly opened the small side window of the twin-engine plane. The cat found the escape it was looking for. Everything went quiet. When the woman realized what had happened, the new screams were so loud it was near impossible to tell Miami Departure that they were returning and even harder to assure them there was no emergency onboard.

On one embarrassing occasion, the guys were waiting to give me a good-natured hard time as "the lost little girl." I had delivered a passenger to Tampa in the morning. On my return flight that afternoon, I found the scattered cloud cover growing denser, obscuring all the ground waypoints I had used flying north. Expecting only the scattered clouds predicted for the day, I hadn't filed an instrument flight plan. I tried to call to file one in flight, but I got no response—my radios were dead. When I tried to tune the navigation radios to a nearby station, I found them useless as well. It was as if the entire world had disappeared from sight and sound, leaving me all alone, deserted in the sky.

While I was in training, I wondered how I would handle an actual emergency. Would I stay calm or panic? I don't think we ever know the answer to such questions about ourselves until the moment occurs. And this was one of those moments. Knowing fear can cause one to overlook the obvious answers, I took deep breaths while carefully double checking everything.

I methodically checked circuit breakers and control knobs as I used the one instrument I could trust, the wet compass. I turned east, knowing from experience the clouds often stop at the coastline. Saying a silent prayer and wishing I had filled the fuel tanks in Tampa, I noticed the clouds thinning. There, just below my wing, I saw the answer, a runway. I had no idea at what airport. I set the transponder to 7600, the signal for loss of communication, and made a radio call on 121.5 with the hope that it was received. Switching to 122.8, the Unicom frequency that all airplanes use at uncontrolled fields, I announced my intentions over the radio, again hoping someone would hear it. I circled down through the hole in the clouds that had seemed to open just for me and entered the traffic pattern to land on the single runway. People came running out of the lone building on the field to meet me, asking if I was the lost little girl.

Unwilling to quibble over technicalities of not being a little girl nor lost—even though I didn't know where I was—I said, "sure," with a shrug. They told me the Tamiami airport thirty miles south had also received the radio calls. An instructor was on the way to save me.

Upon his arrival, my rescuer also failed to get the radios in my plane to work, so we left the plane for repair. Even though it wasn't my fault, I had to suffer the good-natured ribbing as the story was retold with wild variations. In an attempt to change the "little girl" image, I later tried talking in a lower voice on the radio only to be asked why I was trying to sound sexy. Sometimes, there was just no winning.

On another occasion, I again found myself wishing I had refueled when I had the opportunity, but this time was more ominous. After delivering passengers to Nassau, I had to file paperwork in the airport office to leave. I was trying to speed up the process because I had to be home before sundown. A female pilot was a novelty to the people filing my return flight plan and their questions caused it to take much longer than expected. I knew I hadn't used half my fuel on the flight over, so I chose to leave as soon as possible without topping off the fuel tanks. Halfway home, over the Bermuda Triangle, where communication and navigation radios go dead, I noticed the fuel gauges resting on E. My breathing stopped, and my heart raced. I stared at the round dials, willing them to move. Could they be broken? I was grasping at straws, knowing that wasn't the answer.

After a deep breath and again reminding myself that panic does no good, I took stock of the situation. I needed a plan. Turning back wasn't the answer. Who, I wondered, had decided that the best place to store the life vests and raft was behind the back seat? It would be impossible to reach them until after ditching in the ocean. My mind raced. There was no popped circuit breaker. Maybe I had a fuel leak. Could the gauges be wrong? There had to be fuel, or the engines would have stopped.

Then I noticed the L and R on each of the gauges. That reminded me that this plane had two fuel tanks for each engine—four in total, but only two gauges. Each gauge served two tanks. I could breathe again, and my heartbeat returned to normal. With a flip of a switch, the needles moved to F, and all was fantastic.

I once agreed to a flying assignment for the Navy. I was to fly all night at fifty feet over the water, circling a specific area near the coast, watching for a beacon and listening for a radio signal coming from submerged devices that warned of incoming enemy submarines. The instructions were to fly for two hours, land for a one-hour break, and repeat until sunrise. The third time going out, I was beginning to feel tired. When my chin hit my chest, I looked up to see the plane way too close to the water. The adrenaline shock was enough to make me call it quits before dawn.

Some things were just not worth the flight hours or pay. Flying drugs fell into that category. The Everglades were dotted with abandoned planes that had arrived overweight with illegal substances in the middle of the night to be met by the next link in the drug chain. Evidently, the drugs were worth enough to leave the plane behind.

Some of my Carib pilot friends found jobs at a historic part of the Miami airport called Corrosion Corner. The United States Air Force parked C-118s there beside cargo DC-6s from around the world. There were also C-46s, two-radial-engine propeller planes left over from WWII, and the two-engine tail-dragger DC-3. Cargo carriers like Corsair, Rich Aviation, Bahamas Air, Zantop, Airlift, Air Haiti, and Ryan Air used these planes to transport cargo to Central and South America and the Caribbean Islands. A few pilots were lucky enough to fly the airlines' DC-8s, logging precious jet time.

Pilots hungry for flight hours vied for the positions and came back with thrilling stories. Baseballs going to Puerto Rico, where the covers would be handsewn, could play havoc with a plane's critical weight and balance if they came loose from their netting restraints and rolled around with every move of the plane. Hauling cattle could also cause weight and balance issues if they got loose. Other problems arose if the cattle's urine seeped through the protective flooring cover to corrode control cables.

Some pilots preferred the routine of transporting people in smaller, newer planes, like the Martin 404 at Marco Island Airways. Humans, however, could sometimes cause even more problems than baseballs or cattle. Every flight, no matter the plane, cargo, or destination was an adventure and story to share.

There seemed to be a personality type drawn to the profession or created by the demands of aviation. I could never decide which—most likely, it was a combination. The pilots I met had a strong desire for order, structure, and planning in their lives but an even deeper need for adventure, and a longing to be challenged by the unpredictable. They felt compelled to face unknown, unpredictable, and potentially life-threatening situations. To be bored was death itself, so better to live life on the edge or not at all. Requirements for survival included knowledge, training, awareness, self-confidence, acceptance of one's limitations, as well as respect for the machine and weather. Most of my fellow pilots were introverts but enjoyed the company and gathering of friends.

Flying created a type of self-imposed rite of passage that society failed to offer. Logbook entries were testimony to not only the accumulation of hours and knowledge gained but also the personal growth and self-confidence that resulted and followed one through life.

One of the best side benefits of flying was being around other pilots, with their passion, shared language, attitude, view of life, and, therefore, of death. Although no one dwelled on it, we all knew people who had died doing what they loved. It was accepted as part of the deal, making the work and life itself that much more precious and exciting. It was agreed that you don't truly live life to its fullest until you accept death.

We were of the age and culture where drugs and alcohol were available and common, but none of the young pilots I knew abused either. I don't think it was from a sense of self-denial as much as that flight became the drug of choice. The adrenaline rush provided the high and the resulting addiction to the sport. Flying took one-hundred-percent concentration, leaving any worries and problems behind for the time being—mission accomplished. Usually seen as a solo activity, the people who enjoyed flying were gregarious, and when on the ground, they sought out one another's company. Adventures in the sky that only another pilot could understand forged an unspoken bond. I was accepted as one of them, earning the right to tell and listen to the stories of flying drama and humor, all shared in the camaraderie of the TAC-Air Coffee Shop.

14

I Fly a 747!

While butterfly leaves of absence gave me half the year off in Miami to take and give flying lessons, the other half was spent as a flight attendant earning a living to support my flying habit. I found I was a much better, happier flight attendant with this routine. The two worlds both involved aviation and sometimes blended into each other— like the day I got to fly a 747.

Thankfully, in addition to the ten percent turkey factor of guys in TWA's cockpits, there were ninety percent "good guys" who were kind, polite, helpful, and supportive. Within minutes of entering their space, I could tell whether it would be an evening of talking about airplanes like adults or one that that made use of my Child Psych classes. Although I had the seniority to work a different position, to the relief of the other flight attendants, I continually agreed to tend to the pilots. In return, on the rare occasion that the pilots invited me to join them for the take-off or landing, the cabin crew covered my duties with the passengers. I liked being up at the top of the spiral staircase where the magic happened. I loved seeing creation from seven miles up, taking off on a cloudy day, quickly emerging above the overcast layer to a world of sunshine and blue skies, riding on top of the fluffy mounds that gave way as we skimmed their tops. I had seen the Alps painted pink with the paintbrush of sunrise and a runway suddenly appear just seconds after emerging from the thick London fog on an instrument approach. I would allow myself to imagine the impossible: having the cockpit as my workplace.

The good guys welcomed me into their space and their world of aviation knowledge. Some took me along on walk-arounds, the visual inspection before each flight, pointing out the items of interest. One time they even let me fly!

It was a beautiful clear day with smooth air. With a light passenger load, we finished the service quickly, and I took the pilots their after-dinner coffees. I admired Greenland's view covered in ice and snow with blue lakes and rivers flowing to the sea, while Iceland, next door, was much greener. I wondered, again, how or why the names were reversed. Legend has it that one was to lure settlers, the other to deter them.

I was seated in my favorite spot, the raised jump seat behind the captain, where I had a clear view of the cockpit as well as the world. Captain Andrews, one of my favorite pilots, pushed his chair back, unbuckled his seat harness, and stood to leave the cockpit.

"Why don't you enjoy the view from the front row?"

I smiled my thanks as I slid into the warmed seat and adjusted it to fit my shorter frame, moving the chair as far forward and as high as possible. I instinctively put one hand on the yoke in front of me and the other on the throttles to my right, spreading my fingers to rest easily in the smooth indentations. Because the guys sometimes invited me to sit in their seats when they left, the offer wasn't a complete surprise, but what happened next was.

"You want to see how this baby flies?" asked David, the F/O (first officer), to my right. The "baby" was the 747 taking us to Paris that evening. I wasn't sure if it was the beginning of a conversation, a joke, or an unbelievable offer. David, and his wife, Tracy, also a flight attendant, were friends and knew of my flying jobs in Miami. That evening, Tracy and I were trading off serving first class and the cockpit. David was a nice guy but also a jokester. I hesitated to say my ready answer of "You bet" aloud. I didn't want to get suckered in for his idea of fun at my expense.

With no answer forthcoming, David said, "Well, if you do, push the little red button by your thumb twice to turn off the autopilot and the horn."

So I did.

As David played instructor, I made shallow turns left and right, climbed, and then descended just a few hundred feet in each direction, getting the feel of the enormous plane.

"Small movements will do it. She's sensitive—like women."

I was much too preoccupied to react or take exception to David's sexist remark. I had learned by now the best way to deal with the guys' comments was not to take any of it personally and to let it go.

"Try using just two fingers. Apply a bit of back pressure to make her climb. Just release it to come down. If it feels heavy, use the trim button by your other thumb. But again, just the slightest touch will be enough."

I was listening but staring at the instruments, practicing my visual scan, willing them to hold perfectly still to show straight and level flight. At thirty-seven thousand feet, in the ultra-thin air, it wasn't easy to do—it's the reason the pilots use the autopilot once they get to cruising altitude. I tried to relax my grip a bit and found that looking out the front window to use the horizon as a reference, made flying straight and level easier than using the instruments—just like in the Cessna.

David's instructions to change direction and altitude caused just enough of a deviation from what ATC (air traffic control) had assigned that it wouldn't get radar's attention, but it was taking all of mine. My body and mind were absorbed in complying with David's orders. My vision narrowed again to include only the instruments on the panel before me. She is sensitive, I thought, feeling I was getting to know her. I liked that planes, like ships, were referred to in the feminine. She was a sweetie—a big, beautiful, sweet flying machine.

It reminded me of getting to know the horses I grew up riding, how my wishes and commands transferred through my hands and legs to signal the desired movements as we became one entity. I recalled my horse looking back at me as if to say, "If you don't know what you're doing, get off." Planes, like my horses, didn't appreciate ineptitude and were even less forgiving of mistakes. When handled with knowledge and care, however, they provided the same freedom of feeling and movement.

I noticed a bit of delay, a lag in time, between giving the input via the controls and receiving the requested response. I had to be patient, wait for her to give me what I wanted. If I grew impatient and asked for more too quickly, it ended up being too much, and then I had to go in the opposite direction. She was giving me a lesson to be calm under pressure and use her rhythm.

Noticing an altitude loss when I turned, I was ready to push the throttles forward when I felt them move under my fingers. Seeing my surprise, David explained. "Auto throttles take care of that." He quickly added, "And in a jet, the rudder input is done automatically in a turn. So, keep your feet on the floor." He accentuated his words by pointing at my feet and then smiled as I quickly complied, sat up straight, and issued a "Yes, sir."

All was quiet except the four Pratt and Whitney jet engines' muffled roar, so far aft that the cockpit was much quieter than in other commercial jets. Outside, the sky was rapidly growing dark as we flew east, away from the setting sun. The last rays of light reflected pink, orange, and gold on the clouds in the distance. The first stars showed as faint small dots of light high above. The instruments, sensing the fading light, lit up from inside, giving the small room a soft glow.

In *Skyfaring*, by Mark Vanhoenaker (Vintage 2016), I read "There are times in flying when the rest of the world seems to go away, when we seem completely detached from ourselves, our lives, and even from our own ordinary consciousness. Those are the times when we seem to be existing in an intense and dynamic relationship with all that is around us." It's how I felt as I flew that 747. But the sensation lasted for only a moment—until David's voice broke into my reverie.

"OK. I've got it." David took the controls and reengaged the autopilot. I reluctantly removed my hands from the yoke and throttles but couldn't take the smile off my face.

"That was amazing. Thank you so much," was all I could think to say.

"A bit different from those light twins, huh? It's a shame girls can't fly these babies, but I'm sure you understand why."

I had spent quite a bit of time contemplating that very thing, and no, I didn't understand why. I had watched the cockpit crews at work enough to see through the mystique. No magic or super-human act was going on. These were normal, mortal men, some with less education and a lower IQ than mine, in control of a machine that reacted to normal physics and mechanics. I had accepted the all-male world as reality and assumed there must be some good, yet-to-be-revealed reason, or else women would be in that seat already.

No, I don't understand at all, I thought.

I sat silently, not wanting to ruin the magical moment.

When the extended quiet became too awkward, Ben, the flight engineer, jumped in with the answer.

"Well, you know there is just such a difference in the physical ability that is needed—and then the psychological and emotional state, of course."

I turned to look at him, expecting one of those "gotcha" smiles following a joke or an honest answer that made sense. But he was serious. That was the real answer in 1976.

He felt the need to explain further.

"And, you know, especially during that time of the month."

I've never been good at keeping my inner thoughts off my face. The look I shot Ben caused him to sit back in his seat and glance away. Just in time, Captain Andrews opened the door to reenter the cockpit, breaking the uncomfortable silence. I took it as my cue to get out of his seat, express my gratitude, and allow the cockpit to return to normal.

I, on the other hand, would take some time to return to normal. I had just flown a 747!

Image courtesy of TWA Museum

15

Breaking News

I left the cockpit and checked on the passengers enjoying the upstairs cocktail lounge. The 747 was unique with this space for first-class passengers' use during flight as a major part of its marketing message. Pan Am offered restaurant-style dining, American Airlines had baby grand pianos, and TWA featured large, stuffed benches and swivel chairs around conversation tables and an open bar. The concept was very well received by the passengers.

I refilled the bowls of peanuts and pretzels on the small tables. Jerry, another flight attendant from first class, was tending bar and laughing with an attractive passenger. He seemed to have it all under control, so I descended the stairs and found Tracy relaxing in the galley. I considered Tracy to be TWA's version of the ideal flight attendant with her professional hairdo, manicured nails, matching nail polish and lipstick, carefully applied makeup and tasteful jewelry that complimented her petite figure in our new uniform.

I glanced at my nails, remembering my plan to apply nail polish during the commute up from Miami, but it had been a rough ride and I had read instead. My fingers bore evidence of my week's activities working on airplanes and cars. I made a mental note to reapply lipstick after eating this time. My supervisor had recently reprimanded me after she received what was intended to be a "lilac letter," a compliment, from a gentleman who wanted to commend the airline on my "fresh, clean, smiling face void of overdone makeup." Instead, the letter was deemed an "onion letter," a complaint. I received a reprimand and a reminder of proper professional appearance and conduct. I was also reminded yet again that a smile is part of the uniform.

On the previous flight, a male passenger stopped me as I walked down the aisle and said, "Aren't you supposed to be wearing a smile. It makes you so much prettier." I had been concentrating on four drink orders, the corresponding seat numbers, and the promise to heat a baby bottle. I wondered if my male coworkers were ever critiqued for not smiling enough.

It was a bit of a culture shock and challenge to switch from pilot to flight attendant and back again, but I enjoyed both worlds and jobs. When we flew together, Tracy filled me in on what I had missed at TWA when I was away on my latest small plane flying adventures. That night, we were about to begin the exchange when abruptly, the galley curtain opened.

Lewis and Ray, two flight attendants working the coach cabin, joined us in the small space. Lewis was a classmate from my initial training class who had remained a friend. He was among the first male flight attendants TWA hired and the first openly gay person I ever met. Lewis was tall and extremely thin, with carefully styled brown hair, a quick wit, a constant smile, and boundless energy. The passengers loved him. He was as city as I was country and served as a continual source of information for me. Soon after graduation, we worked a flight together to Shannon, Ireland where he explained the importance of having matching patterns for table place settings. I had no need for china nor desire to collect crystal and silver, and I thought patterns were for cutting out material to sew a dress. We both found the other highly entertaining.

After completing his service duties on flights, Lewis crocheted dresses that he sold for thousands of dollars to New York boutiques. The flight attendant gig was just to feed his desire for travel. Ray, his new partner, was quieter and more serious but equally kind. They flew together whenever possible. They couldn't wait to share the latest stories from the back—the unruly children with sleeping parents, the drunk in 28C buying drinks for the lady next to him, the pet ferret whose owner kept taking it out of the cage, and the couple trying to join the "mile high club" causing the line for the bathroom to grow long enough to block the aisle.

Lewis turned to Tracy and me to ask in a hushed tone, "So, how are things up here?"

"Fine as far as I know," Tracy answered. "Carol finished here and went to help out in the back; Jerry is tending bar in the lounge; and Lynn's been taking care of the guys upstairs."

Turning to me, she asked, "Are the boys behaving themselves?"

"Yeah," I answered with a pause, wondering how much to share. "Actually, they're being very nice."

"Well, better you than me, girl," chimed in Lewis, turning from his plate of cheese and apple to pat my shoulder.

"Yes, thank you," added Ray, also preparing a plate to take to the back to eat. As the most junior crew member, he would have likely been assigned to the cockpit had I not volunteered. The awful treatment male flight attendants received from some of the cockpit crews was legendary. Some pilots would ban them from the cockpit, refuse to acknowledge their existence, tease them, or make even ruder comments than they did to the women.

"These guys are OK, especially your sweet husband, David," I said, smiling at Tracy. I was dying to share my amazing, best-thing-that-ever-happened-to-me experience and rationalized that he would probably tell his wife anyway, so I continued.

"In fact, you'll never guess what they let me do."

Hearing the excitement in my voice, all three glanced up from their plates, waiting.

"I got to fly the plane!"

"What do you mean?" Lewis asked, wrinkling his brow.

"Captain Andrews let me sit in his seat, and David let me fly."

"You moved the steering wheel?" Ray was trying to understand.

"It's the yoke, but yeah. I turned left and right, up and down. Not enough that Air Traffic Control or even you guys probably noticed."

"I did." Lewis piped up. "I thought we were going around clouds. It was very smooth." He smiled his approval.

I turned to Tracy. "So, tell your honey that I said thanks."

"He loves instructing, so I'm sure he enjoyed it too. I bet you were good. You're an instructor and fly charters, don't you? It's just not fair that women can't be airline pilots."

"But now they can," Ray said.

"Small planes, yes, but not for the airlines," Tracy explained.

Lewis jumped in.

"No, the airlines, too. Our friend Roger flies for American, and he said they have a female pilot now."

"Are you sure?" I asked, knowing that he must have heard it wrong.

"I can ask him again, but I'm pretty sure that's what he said."

"Would you please? And ask which plane he's talking about and if he can find her name."

"You know I will." Lewis gave me a peck on the cheek and peeked through the curtain into the coach cabin.

"We better go. The natives are getting restless."

First class seating with spiral staircase leading
to upper deck lounge and cockpit

First class upstairs lounge

Main cabin divided into 4 sections with ten seats across and two aisles with seating for over four hundred.

TWA's 747 interior in 1972 .Courtesy of Boeing Co.

16

Mentors

By the time I saw Lewis again, I had confirmed the female airline pilot rumor. Not one, but two women had joined the sixty thousand male commercial airline pilots by 1976. Three years earlier, Frontier Airlines, then a scheduled regional carrier, had hired Emily Howell and already upgraded her to captain on a Twin Otter. That same year, American was the first major airline to hire a female for the flight deck: Bonnie Tiburzi.

If this were true, why wasn't it headline news? Why had I always been told women could never and would never be airline pilots? If these women could make it, could I? I wondered how they did it. What did they possess that made it possible? Finally, I quit wondering and wrote a letter to each of them via their airlines.

Both responded to my questions with a similar message. According to my new mentors, my size, age, and college major were not a factor. Women were just as capable of flying a commercial jet as any man. As a flight attendant, they each reminded me, I already had a good idea of the lifestyle and work environment—primary considerations in choosing the career. Bonnie added a prescient warning. Some male pilots, she foretold, may not be pleased with a woman "causing trouble" by trying to join their ranks. Her response, she told me, was that she had no intention of making trouble; she just wanted to make a living as they did. Both letters encouraged me to continue flying to increase my flight hours and experience. They wished me well on my quest to join them as professional airline pilots.

I read the letters over and over. This changed everything. If they could do this, so could I. The "truths" and "facts" I had been told were actually lies. The news and encouragement in those letters changed my world and future in a way very few other events ever had or would.

I needed many more flight hours, plus written and flight exams passed, before I could even think about filling out airline applications. Goals and dreams I had thought impossible—forbidden even—were now within my reach. I just didn't know the next steps.

Because most of my fellow aviators at the New Tamiami Airport shared the same dream of being hired by a major airline, news of available flying jobs was a constant topic of conversation. Convinced I had reached as far as I could go as a pilot, I hadn't paid much attention. I loved my life and was content—until now.

Knowing there might be options and possibilities out there, I began listening more carefully, asking questions, and doing research. The airline industry was highly cyclical, and most of the airlines had not hired pilots during the early seventies. The backlog of candidates already on file plus all the new hopefuls allowed them to set their highest hiring requirements. To be competitive, TWA applicants had to be younger than thirty and have a four-year college degree, a completed flight engineer written exam, an ATP (airline transport pilot) certificate, 1500 hours of total flight time, 1000 hours of jet time, and 1000 hours of PIC (pilot-in-command) time. Meeting those demands seemed insurmountable and undoable. I was twenty-four and had a college degree, but the rest felt beyond my reach except the flight engineer written exam.

Sam and Tom talked about a class they were looking forward to in their last semester of the career pilot program. It met in the evenings and prepared them to take the flight engineer written exam. When I showed interest in going, too, they invited me along.

The nervousness I felt walking into the classroom disappeared when I met the instructor, John Archibald, with his warm smile, informal dress, and casual attitude. He listened attentively as I explained that I only wanted to monitor the class, that I already had a bachelor's degree in education from the University of Illinois, and now I had an interest in aviation. Pleading my case, I went on to say that I had all my flight licenses and ratings and was a certificated instructor, instructing at the same FBO with Sam and Tom and many of his other students. He seemed easily persuaded and happy to have me.

"Well, that's all just fine," he said when I finished. "Sit wherever you like, and feel free to ask questions. That's how we learn."

He returned to writing a list of words on the blackboard. I joined my friends in the back row of the small classroom. Gradually, it filled with young men hoping for a future in aviation. No one seemed to notice or care that I was there.

Being the only female in the room was nothing new. As a tomboy growing up, I preferred horseback riding to dress-up and often found it more fun to play the boys' games at recess. I was the only girl to take shop in high school, learning to solder and weld. I was the only female student and instructor at the flight school. So, my gender wasn't the cause for my discomfort in the class—it was the material.

Despite Mr. Archibald's hospitable manner, within the first few minutes of the class, I knew I had made a mistake. I had no idea what he was talking about as he went down the list of terms on the blackboard. I had never heard of an electromagnetic generator, hydraulic accumulator, differential pressure, anti-ice, fuel heat, mix valves, PSI, APU, ACM, EGT, or a host of other three-letter combinations. "Busses" was the only word in the list that sounded familiar, but I was sure it had nothing to do with transportation. As the new student and only girl, I didn't dare raise my hand, especially when everyone else seemed to understand.

When class finally ended, I waited until everyone was gone to thank Mr. Archibald for offering me the opportunity and then added that I didn't want to waste his time. I admitted that I had understood nothing. As he erased the mystery words on the blackboard, he looked at me over his shoulder. Maintaining the same kind, engaged demeanor he had while lecturing, he surprised me with his response.

"Oh, you'll be okay. No one else in here knows all of this either. It was a general overview of everything we will learn this semester in preparation for the exam. It always seems like a lot to everyone at first. I guarantee you aren't the only one to leave here feeling overwhelmed."

It was nice of him to try, but I knew my limitations. "I'm not ready for this level. They have had one and a half years leading up to this. None of it makes any sense to me."

To my astonishment, Mr. Archibald was the one not willing to give up, offering to take on the challenge to mentor me. "If you will come in one hour before each class and are willing to do some reading, I could help you catch up and be prepared for what I will teach that night."

Seeing the weight of defeat and embarrassment still there, he continued. "Just try it at least once. If you find it helps, we can continue. Let's not quit just yet."

I couldn't believe it. Not only was he going to allow me into the class, but he would provide private tutoring. He was the one arguing for me to keep trying.

"Okay, I guess," I replied, trying to sound less despondent.

"Great!" he exclaimed, putting down the eraser and reaching for his briefcase. "See you Wednesday."

I soon discovered that teaching was Mr. Archibald's second career. He had first worked as a mechanic at Eastern Airlines. When the disruption of strikes and ongoing union versus management tension took all the enjoyment out of the job, he got a degree in education. With his A&P (airframe and powerplant) license, experience as a mechanic, access to the parts department, and passion for teaching, his class in 727 systems was a favorite among aspiring airline pilots.

True to his word, Mr. Archibald met with me before each class to explain that evening's subject matter. He would often bring a part with him from the actual plane that I could see and touch to understand better.

On that first Wednesday, he brought in the primary energy source for almost every system on a jet plane—the jet engine.

"It's really quite simple," he began. "And a thing of beauty."

His expression showed appreciation for the men and their discoveries that had gone into this invention. He saw engineering and mechanics as art forms that he loved to explain, and I was the incredibly fortunate recipient.

"As you know, the car and the small airplanes you're flying now use reciprocating engines with spark plugs making timed explosions inside pistons that turn the car's axle or the plane's prop.

Well, they came up with a much better, easier, and simpler idea with fewer moving parts for the jet engine. It just has this shaft with blades and a ring of these cans."

He pointed to the parts lying on the table.

"A jet engine has a continuous explosion going on inside a ring of these burner cans."

He held up an oblong can about the size of a football with holes in it.

"The ring of cans is placed around this shaft," he said, holding up a short pole with a series of small fan blades on both ends.

He pointed to each component as he went through his demonstration. "Ignitor plugs go in one of the holes on each can, and fuel injector nozzles go in the other. The fuel vaporizes in the air inside the can, explodes with ignition, and then just keeps burning at a constant rate. The expanding hot air escapes out the exhaust, propelling the aircraft forward. As it leaves, it blows by these turbine blades, causing them to spin, which turns the shaft, causing the blades on the front, called compressor blades, to turn. That pulls in more air and compresses it to feed to the combustion cans, and it keeps itself going."

He took a minute to catch his breath. I, too, was in awe of the simple beauty of the machine as well as the teacher who could explain it in such an articulate, easy-to-understand way.

"It's a self-perpetuating system. Or, as you'll hear the boys explain the process," he added with a wry smile, "Suck, Squeeze, Bang, and Blow."

I took it as an indication that I was accepted as one of the guys.

He explained that in addition to being propulsion for the plane, various parts of the jet engine and the attached accessory gearbox are the sources for most of the airplane's systems. The rotating shaft creates the magnetic field for the electromagnetic generator to produce and provide electricity. It also runs the hydraulic pump that sends fluid to the control surfaces, gear, and brakes. The heated, denser air from the compressor section heats and pressurizes the plane and prevents ice forming on the plane's surfaces.

On other evenings, Mr. Archibald produced an air-cycle machine, a hydraulic pump and actuator, fuel pump, lock-out disc brakes, and other system parts. I learned how alternating current (AC) and voltage could be changed to direct current (DC) with a transformer rectifier (TR)—and finally, the definition of busses. It turns out they are electrical distribution centers. So many amazing facts about my everyday world were completely new to me. With the help of Mr. Archibald's show-and-tell technique, together with his sketched diagrams, the airplane came alive. I began to understand the source, destination, and use of the fluids, air, and energy that ran through her.

Like Mr. Archibald, I began to see the plane as a piece of art, a thing of beauty. I, too, was in awe of the minds who created it, but also of the personalities who could explain how it worked and teach it. As a teacher myself, I think I appreciated the gift he had more than his other students. Mr. Archibald was a natural teacher, enthusiastic but patient, extremely knowledgeable but humble, never condescending. and thrilled to see his students finally getting it. He was one of those amazing human beings who love to impart their knowledge and find joy in those "aha" moments when the student finally gets it.

As our college semester came to an end, we studied for the final: the FAA flight engineer written exam. A sample test study guide included five times the questions that would be asked and took weeks to complete, but ultimately it prepared the student well. Sam and I studied together every chance we had, quizzing each other until we completed the guide flawlessly. I couldn't remember ever working so hard or studying that much for any class or enjoying it more.

At TWA, I chose to work flights on the Boeing 727 and took my books to study on trips. Toward the end of the semester, each student had the opportunity to sit in a 727 simulator to see and touch the flight engineer panel. I alone had the added benefit of spending time in a real 727 cockpit. Most TWA flight engineers were encouraging and willing to help explain the material in the study questions. They thought it cute that I was so interested in their job that I would study to take the exam for the license, and even congratulated me when I passed it with one of the highest grades in the class. However, they were quick to remind me that I would never use that new precious ticket that I had worked for so hard. After all, real airline pilots came from the military where MEN could get the required jet time and proper training.

Sometimes my questions became a source of fun for them, telling the flight engineer he should switch places with me.

"Hey, Joe. I think she knows more about that panel than you. Why don't you let her sit there, and you go pour coffee? She's a lot nicer to look at, too," they might say with a wink.

I was reminded once again of my proper place in the grand scheme of things and left wondering whether it would ever change.

Mr. Archibald 40 years later

17

Wanted: Jet Time

A few TWA pilots understood my dream and took it seriously enough to try to help me with suggestions. Most had obtained their flying experience in the military, so initially, they encouraged me to try the same route. However, the first obstacle was my age. At twenty-four, I was too old to give the military the required seven-year commitment and still be hirable by the airlines who wanted pilots younger than thirty. In talks with recruiters, I found that the age issue didn't matter since no branch of the military trained women as pilots.

Another helpful suggestion was to contact the Air National Guard, which flew military jets and hired "weekend warriors." Many of the guys who shared my desire to fly but had no funds trained with the Air National Guard or were in the Reserve. I liked the idea—it would give me the experience and background for the airlines and an extra paycheck after I got out in return for staying available for national emergencies. It sounded perfect until I talked to the local Long Island recruiter who explained that they also didn't accept female applicants. Their aviation recruits had to be capable of being assigned to either cargo or fighter aircraft. Since women were prohibited from combat duty in 1977, their options and usefulness were limited. The military solution was to not let them apply.

"However," one sympathetic recruiter added over the phone, "there has to be a way for you to do this. It's not right, you know. Many women are as good pilots as men. Some even flew in the war. My girlfriend told me about a new organization that helps women with these kinds of legal issues to make sure they are treated fairly. I bet they would help with your legal fees if you sued for your rights. I think it's called NOW."

"That's a great idea," I said, grasping at the small nugget of hope. I, too, had heard of the National Organization for Women, mostly about burning bras and having marches with signs. I had no idea how to contact them.

The thought of applying to the military triggered an inner philosophical debate. Could I, in good conscience, argue to receive government-paid training that I wanted to use only for my personal purposes? I had taken part in protests, marches, and sit-ins on the Illinois campus during the Vietnam War. I believed the U.S. was in the wrong. Like many others, I was against war in theory. I supposed if it were to protect my family, country, and way of life, I would fight and use my training, but was I being honest? To argue that I deserved the same rights and opportunities as a man, I would have to be willing to perform in combat as he would. I could argue that he should not have to be there either, but that wasn't up for debate and didn't solve my issue. My parents had been clear about their view, saying people much smarter than I were making the decisions I needed to follow. I considered taking part in the Kent State protest and was hurt when my mother said the students there and I deserved to be shot if we took part. Many changes were going on in the early seventies, and the generation gap was common in families. That night a phone call with my parents resolved my turmoil.

After listening to the latest hometown news and giving them my plans for a visit to Illinois, I wanted to share the idea of how to continue my quest. They were never ones to discourage an idea or quash an adventure, but as realists, they were dubious about my latest pursuit to be a pilot. At age twenty-four, instead of being settled into a teaching career with my student loan paid off and in a promising relationship, I was barely making ends meet working half time as a flight attendant, making five dollars an hour instructing and flying charters, moving like a gypsy between New York and Miami, and living with a younger man equally as poor.

They wished me well, however. My mom, who still lived in the farmhouse where she was born, enjoyed hearing of my flights, visiting my friends, and, I suspected, lived vicariously through me. She also enjoyed the travel privileges available to an airline employee's parents. My German, conservative, Midwest farming father watched my flying pursuits with interest. He shared that he had often dreamed of taking lessons while attending Southern Illinois University, where they had a flight school. He went to college there until the war started and he had to leave university to help on the family farm. Flying was a luxury he could not afford then or later. The one comment I remember he made on the subject was about needing a rich husband.

With both my parents on the phone, I thought it a good time to present my latest great idea. I could picture my mom sitting on a stool at the counter in the kitchen and Dad at his desk.

"I think I have a way to get the jet time I need."

"Oh yeah? How's that?" asked my mother, distracted by something I could hear cooking on the stove.

"Well, I'm too old for the regular military, but if the Reserve or Guard accept me, I could get flight training in the jets, but I'd have to sue. There's an organization called NOW that would maybe help if I...."

My sentence remained unfinished as Dad interrupted.

"Sue who?" he demanded.

"Uh, I guess the U.S. government."

I realized I hadn't asked the recruiter or given the "who" much thought.

"Lynn," Mother interrupted. "You wouldn't take orders when you were two. How in the world would you survive the military?"

Before I could argue, Dad was on again. "You are NOT suing the U.S. government, young lady. I'm sure you can find another way."

And that was the end of it—until one day a few months later when a bizarre series of coincidences provided the answer to my dilemma.

Section III:

I'm an Airline Pilot

18

Air Illinois

With five years of seniority, I could often get a flight schedule that included a layover in St. Louis, just across the Mississippi River from my family's farm in Southern Illinois. I was looking forward to a visit with my sister who lived near Carbondale, Illinois. The two-hour drive to her home followed the Mississippi south along impressive limestone bluffs and gorgeous farmland. I didn't usually like long drives, but that route was an exception.

After the passengers deplaned, I told the rest of the crew my plan and left them waiting for the hotel van. I headed to the car rental counter when serendipity stopped me in my tracks. A sign above a small kiosk caught my eye. It said "Carbondale" with a departure time in ten minutes. Two men in pilot uniforms were chatting with a young woman behind the counter labeled "Air Illinois." They turned their attention to me as I walked up, smiling.

"You have a flight to Carbondale?" I asked, nodding at the sign.

"Sure do. Leaving right now. Want to go?"

"I'd love to. I have a sister there I'd like to visit during my overnight. Do you guys by any chance give airline employee discounts?"

I reached for my employee ID in case being in uniform wasn't enough proof.

In unison, the three shook their heads.

"No. Sorry. The boss doesn't believe in those agreements," said the first officer, speaking for the group. It was obvious they disagreed with the policy. Then he added, "The only time we can give a ride is for an interview."

"Well, I could interview," I countered, half kidding, not yet willing to give up altogether.

"Right now, we have enough flight attendants," the captain responded. "Just always need pilots," he added, to which the others nodded knowingly.

"Okay, then, I'll interview as a pilot."

They didn't seem pleased with what they assumed was pushing a fun chat a bit too far.

"Seriously," I added quickly. "I have over seven hundred hours flying charters and instructing in Florida."

Both pilots looked at me and spoke at once.

"Really?"

"That's more than I had when I got hired."

"What planes are you flying there?"

The captain looked at his watch as he spoke, picked up my crew bag, and began walking toward the elevator. The first officer gathered the paperwork and waved goodbye to the woman behind the counter before catching up with us. The elevator dropped us off on the ground floor. We walked through the employee cafeteria and out to the ramp where a large, high-winged plane with two-propeller engines waited.

"She's a Twin Otter," he said by way of introduction as we got closer. "Fixed landing gear, turboprop engines, and STOL wings."

He was kind enough to continue, explaining what he had just said.

"Turboprops are jet engines with variable pitch propellers, and STOL means short take-off and landing. Propeller planes are more efficient at low altitudes, while jets are better up high. The turboprop gives the best of both worlds for short-distance trips like ours. The STOL wings let her drop like a rock if you need her to and stop in the width of a runway. No pressurization, so we stay below ten thousand feet."

I followed him up the four steps and ducked to enter the cabin. The stairs collapsed when the first officer pulled the door closed. The captain tossed my bag in a small cargo area at the aft of the fifteen-seat passenger cabin. We made our way up the aisle between the passengers reading and waiting patiently. He motioned me to the center seat in the front row, which allowed a clear view into the cockpit. I was almost sitting between the two pilots.

The first thing I noticed was that the throttles were hanging from the ceiling, which I had never seen before. The pilot's panels had the familiar array of radio heads and flight instruments, so I could follow our progress as we flew south.

"It's going to get loud," the first officer said while handing me a heavy headset already plugged into the communication panel by his seat. After putting on the two large ear-coverings connected with a metal headband, I was able to listen to air traffic control and talk with the pilots during the flight.

All the way to Carbondale and between radio calls, I asked questions about the plane and their job at Air Illinois. They said they flew about four or five days each week for six to eight hours a day on either the morning or evening runs. The flights went north as far as Quincy, Illinois, and south to Memphis, Tennessee, with six to eight stops along the way. They liked being home with family every evening, and for some of their peers, it was the best flying job they could hope for. However, my two pilots dreamed of a job with the majors, so they asked lots of questions about TWA, which hadn't hired in over six years.

We circumvented some storms as they discussed the lack of weather radar. Rumor was that one of the three planes in the fleet used to have a radar unit, but after pilots squabbled about who got it when, the owner resolved the issue by pulling it out and putting it on the shelf in the hangar. He sounded like a real peach of a guy.

The forty-five-minute flight was over much too quickly. I thanked the pilots for the ride and their kindness before going inside the small terminal to wait for my sister. Arriving by plane and so much earlier than planned, I would have to wait for her to finish work before coming to get me. As I waited, I began to worry and feel guilty. Those guys were so nice to me. What if they get in trouble? What if someone compared the tickets with the passenger list or the woman in St. Louis told someone?

I approached the lone person at the ticket counter.

"Jennifer," I said quietly, reading her name tag. "Could I please use your telephone for a local call and have an application? I just flew in from St. Louis in hopes of an interview."

I tried to sound casual as I gave her enough information that any blame for the passenger discrepancy could be placed on me. Uninterested in my explanation, Jennifer pointed to the phone on the counter and repeated the same information I had heard in St. Louis.

"We have enough flight attendants right now."

I dialed my sister's work number and left a message asking her to pick me up at the airport and then attempted to continue the conversation with Jennifer.

"Yes, ma'am," I replied, staying patient with the assumption. "I want to apply to be a pilot," which got her attention.

She looked up from her paperwork.

"What?"

I wasn't sure if she was surprised, irritated, or confused by what I had said, so I repeated it again more slowly and calmly. Without saying another word or giving me any indication of what she was thinking, she disappeared into a door behind her. A few moments later, she emerged with an application in her hand and followed by a tall, stern man with a gray military flattop haircut and matching demeanor. He carried a coffee mug with small red pigs between the large letters MCP. Jennifer handed me the application with a look of apology, knowing what was about to transpire.

"So, you think you want to be an airline pilot! Well, ain't that a hoot!?"

The man's booming voice caused everyone in the small terminal to turn and look at me. I could feel my face turning hot and red.

"Yes, sir," I replied, looking up to meet his gaze as he stepped uncomfortably closer.

"Well, let me show you around my airline," he bellowed as he put his arm around my shoulder to guide me out the door. My mortification continued as we walked into the maintenance hangar where men in work jeans stopped what they were doing and stared to see a woman in a place where I had a feeling one had not stood before.

"Vic!" His loud voice echoed in the metal building. "Show the little lady around." With that, Mr. MCP turned sharply on his heel and left. I already felt sorry for Vic.

"It's okay," I said, embarrassed beyond words. "I'm just waiting for my sister, and I can go back inside."

But Vic seemed happy for the distraction from the open engine nacelle. He came over to introduce himself and patiently listened as I told him the events that landed me there. His soft, friendly voice was a welcomed change from his boss's. He was happy to show and explain the inner workings of the turboprop engine open to view. Thanks to Mr. Archibald's class, I was able to ask some intelligent questions and understand the answers. Vic said the airline owner, Mr. Dezondoulet, a former Canadian Air Force commander, was a hard taskmaster and quite proud of his well-earned "Male Chauvinist Pig" title, explaining the coffee mug's MCP with little red pigs.

I was relieved to see my sister's car pull up at the terminal. Jennifer assured me I could turn in my application and have a ride back to St. Louis the next morning. I was sure that was the last I would hear from Air Illinois.

I was astounded to get a call two months later from Jennifer inviting me to a training session starting in two weeks. The last time I saw her, we had a fun time talking and making fun of Mr. MCP while I waited for my flight, so I assumed she was kidding, the most reasonable of the possibilities.

"Jennifer, is this a joke?"

"No, really. There's a training class scheduled just for you."

"Training? As a pilot? For the Otter? You're sure? I've been hired? No interview? No physical? Do you need copies of my licenses or logbook? I just show up in two weeks?"

I was struggling to make sense of what was going on.

"Is there a new owner?"

She answered my string of questions in order.

"Yes, training as a pilot. On the Twin Otter. Ray, our chief pilot, will be your instructor. No, same owner. Mr. D says you two already talked and to tell you to show up. I think you impressed Vic with what you know about planes and engines."

I paused, wondering why I was refusing to believe this and thinking of all the reasons I couldn't go. Finally, I simply stated, "Okay. I'll be there. See you then."

"There will be a ticket waiting for you in St. Louis," said Jennifer, adding, "It will be nice to see you again. We need more women around here."

Only after I hung up did I realize I hadn't asked about salary, benefits, or work schedule, but I knew the answers wouldn't have mattered. After my return to Miami, I had discovered that turboprop time counted as jet time for airline applications, which would complete the requirements for an interview with TWA. I would have willingly taken the job without pay, which is about what it turned out to be.

My flight attendant supervisor, who was almost as excited about my new flying job as I was, helped me get a nine-month leave of absence that would start in six weeks, the best he could do. Between creative bidding, trip trades, sick and vacation days, and going without sleep, I somehow made it work. For several weeks, I worked two full-time jobs—as a pilot and a flight attendant, some days going straight from one role to the other without much sleep. Federal regulations limit pilots' flying time, but there were no such restrictions for flight attendants and no rules against combining the two, although maybe there should have been. Somehow, I managed to stretch myself between the two workplaces and jobs without crashing—figuratively or literally.

Sam, who had found a job flying vintage cargo planes out of Miami's Corrosion Corner, was excited for me as I packed. We shared promises to visit each other as often as possible.

Orientation and ground school in Carbondale were held in a room off the airport café and lasted only one week. Although I hadn't asked, I was expecting a bit more in salary, since the airline pilots I knew made a good living. Captain Ray informed me, in an apologetic tone, that commuter pilot beginning pay was five-hundred dollars per month before taxes and uniform deductions. It was quite a pay cut from my flight attendant job. It would barely cover my living expenses. No wonder there was such a high turnover rate.

Mr. D, the airline owner, made an appearance on the last day of training and quickly reaffirmed his MCP status.

"Well, here you are. You will be treated like all the other crew members and expected to act accordingly. Nothing special."

He glared at me, and I wondered why I had been hired.

"You may have heard. There's another girl here, flying as a captain, older than you. You will not fly together. I'm sure you understand."

I wondered why people kept telling me I should understand something that made no sense. It was his airline, so I guessed he could make whatever rules he wanted and expect people to just understand. Evidently deciding I deserved an explanation, he continued in an irritated tone.

"Well, heaven forbid something happens; a man has to be up there to deal with it. Passengers expect that. And, we don't want to scare anyone away, do we?"

From him, it sounded as if that rationale should be obvious to everyone.

He left, slamming the door behind him. No time for questions or need for discussions as far as he was concerned. We may not be able to fly together, but just the fact that there was another woman, and she was already a captain was *huge* news. So, women could be captains! I couldn't wait to correct my TWA pilot friends.

Ground school was followed by flight training—three touch-and-goes at the airport, stalls, engine failure practice, and a week of line flying with Ray. Official training was complete two weeks after I arrived. The rest would be OJT, on-the-job training. Fortunately, I had very kind, competent captains to show me the ropes and an easy, forgiving plane to fly and land.

I loved flying the Otter and quickly felt at home at the controls. The routes we flew also made me feel at home. Silos dotted the rural landscape and became guideposts on the horizon for our visual flights. After a few months, I knew each farmstead as a neighbor below. Without radar, when the weather got ugly, we did our best to avoid the visible storms and "green air," a phenomenon that turns air surrounding a hailstorm the color of pea soup. We kidded that our definition of flying IFR, which usually means "instrument flight rules," was instead "I follow railroads," as we dropped below the cloud layer to find our way to the next airport visually.

With only two of Air Illinois's three planes in operation at a time, our routes were simple and always started from the Carbondale airport. There were just four variations for the day's schedules: North to St. Louis and Quincy, back to Carbondale, then south to Cape Girardeau, Jonesboro, and Memphis, returning to the same cities on the way back, or go south first and then north. My schedule was either six o'clock in the morning to one in the afternoon or one in the afternoon to eight at night. We usually flew close to the legal limit of one hundred hours each month.

Other than no radar, the main complaint about the flying was the lack of temperature control in the cockpit. All the cooling or heating air was directed aft to the passenger cabin, leaving the pilots dripping in sweat during the summer and flying in ski gear to stay warm during the winter. My winter uniform consisted of long underwear, doubled wool socks inside lined boots, a down jacket, gloves, a neck scarf, and a ski hat over the headset. I arrived at work with a thermos of Morning Thunder tea and my paper bag meal. There was no onboard food service and not enough time during our brief ground stops to get a hot meal nor the funds to spend so extravagantly.

It was months before one of the pilots finally revealed the reason Mr. MCP agreed to hire women. He needed a government loan to add small jets to the fleet. The Equal Employment Opportunity Commission had just been established in 1976, the previous year. He needed minorities. He had two female applicants on file, so problem solved. We were his tokens.

His stipulation preventing the two of us from flying together worked fine until one dark and stormy afternoon. The weather was wet, and the roads to the airport were icy. When no other first officer could get to the airport, the dispatcher called me. I arrived to find Emily in the left seat. The dispatcher called Mr. D to ask what he wanted to do about the full load of passengers waiting to go north.

As thunder rolled and lightning flashed in the background, Mr. D bellowed his answer so loudly I could hear him through the receiver.

"Fine," he boomed, clearly irritated at the situation. "Tell them to take the flight, but keep the door closed. And no one makes any announcements."

That would keep anyone on board from knowing (heaven forbid) that two women, without the help of a man, had flown them safely through the storms to their destination. He would have made us invisible if he could.

Our flight together was routine and without incident. We went about doing our job as we would have with a male crewmember, as professionals.

I guess since no catastrophe occurred and no one refused to board the plane, the ban was lifted. Emily and I had the opportunity to fly together another dozen times during the remaining six months I was at Air Illinois. I brought a camera to one of those flights and took photos of us. I wanted to show the guys at TWA that women could be captains after all. Neither of us thought of it as a historic event at the time. We were just doing our jobs.

However, our first flight together was remarkable in one respect. Captain Emily Jones, First Officer Lynn Rippelmeyer, and Flight Attendant Barbie Hoffman, on December 30, 1977, made history as the first all-female crew of a scheduled airline. *

Twin Otter

My first airline pilot uniform

World's first all-women airline crew

*Emily and I lost track of each other when we left Air Illinois. Over forty years later, on January 7, 2019, we were reunited on a PBS special called *We'll Meet Again* with Ann Curry, available on the PBS website.

19

Too Short to Fly

When my leave of absence from TWA ended in the summer of 1978, I left Air Illinois to return to Miami, Sam, and my job as a flight attendant. I had accumulated the precious jet time that the TWA pilots told me I needed and enough flight hours for an ATP (air transport pilot) license. With more training and a successful ATP check ride, I finally met all the requirements for the TWA pilot application, the most demanding of the airlines.

I sent resumes and applications requesting an interview to every airline, including the biggies—Pan Am, Eastern, Braniff, United, Delta, American, Continental, and of course, my favorite, TWA. I included Ozark because it was based in St. Louis and close to home.

In 1978, the hiring drought that lasted most of the seventies was finally over. My flying friends were excited and hopeful about being in the right place at the right time in the uncertain industry. Many were hoping the larger, heavier DC-3, DC-6, and C-46 time found at Corrosion Corner would be as valuable as the smaller aircraft turboprop and jet time and that a two-year degree would be enough, as it had in the past during pilot shortages. Because aviation and the hiring process were so unpredictable, it was hard to know. I hoped that the door Bonnie and Emily had opened would be ajar for me.

I was unaware at the time of the 1976 court decree requiring United to increase its hiring of minorities and women, which prompted other airlines to follow suit. I likewise was unaware that some other airlines didn't require a college degree, jet time, or the ATP certificate that TWA did.

Responses came in the mail inviting me to the first stage of the airlines' multi-step interview process. Information spread among applicants full of hints, cautions, and rumors for the prospective interviewee. United had the most extensive process with five stages. American and Delta seemed the least hopeful for non-military. At Delta, the interviewee sat in a rocking chair while answering questions posed by a shrink. To rock or not to rock—that was the question.

Every pilot can recall the interview that launched a career or dashed their hopes. I started preparing, planning, and practicing. How could I best answer the questions I was sure they would ask? How much make-up should I wear? Hair up or down? Heels or flats? Smiling and friendly, or serious and business-like? What should I wear to look professional yet feminine, attractive but not sexy, competent but not competitive? Where was that fine line between pleasant but not the distraction some pilots were already complaining that women in the cockpit would be? With all the attention to looks, I almost forgot my logbook, the only crucial accessory.

The interviews were held at the airlines' main offices. It was apparent at each that women were not expected. The bus drivers picking up candidates from the assigned parking lots refused to stop for me, pointing to the bus coming for the flight attendant hopefuls. When I managed to get on, insisting that it was the correct bus and refusing to get off, my driver made a special stop at the flight attendant interview location anyway. I learned to show up extra early to be sure I ultimately arrived on time for the correct interview.

Waiting rooms for the interviewees were always interesting. Male applicants who filled them all must have read *Dress for Success* and gone to the same barber to get just the right combination of military and modern-day trim to pass inspection but not look weird in the civilian world. The clones sat silently clutching briefcases that carried the precious logbooks recording their flying history. I always started a conversation with whichever guy next to me looked the friendliest. I figured I could at least spend the time educating some male pilots that there *were* qualified females out there and get a feel for what kind of pilot that airline preferred. It often broke the ice and caused others to talk and enjoy the wait more.

Airline interviews were all reasonably similar, conducted by a combination of pilots and employees from the human resources department. The first stage was a logbook and resume fact check of whether applicants met the minimum requirements and verification of no "Parker pen time"—hours logged but not flown. The second stage was a personality check, a conversation with the interviewers, to see if the candidate would fit in. Along the way was a battery of memory, psychological, spatial intelligence, multi-tasking tests, and sometimes a simulator ride to check flying skills. The final stage was a physical that included a full chest x-ray and EKG.

I tested well and enjoyed the challenge but was concerned about some of the questions that inevitably came up. They always asked if a family member had flown or been in the military. When my answer was no, it seemed to short circuit the next battery of questions they expected to ask. Likewise, my honest answer to "Have you always wanted to be a pilot?" had to be no, since I had not considered it an option as a child. When I mentioned that I tried to sign up for aviation classes in college only to learn no girls were allowed in the class, awkward silence followed. Remembering riding my horse to the limestone overhang of the bluffs where I would imagine Lucky sprouting Pegasus-like wings to soar over the farmlands below, I could truthfully reply, "I've always wanted to fly."

To complement their question about any military background as best I could, I explained that I had considered the military, but at the age of twenty-four, I was too old to fulfill the seven-year military commitment and still be younger than thirty for the airlines. I had also tried the Reserves and Air National Guard, but neither trained female pilots. My father had ruled out asking the National Organization for Women to sue the US government.

My pre-solo flight hours were also a significant concern. Ten hours was the norm; I had over sixty. The military trained to proficiency, using as few lessons as necessary. That left the general impression that the best pilots required the fewest training hours.

I wondered how to explain that my flying was just a fun way for my instructors and me to spend the summer; that I had found something I loved to do at every opportunity with people kind enough to teach me. It never occurred to me that all those hours of fun would come back to haunt me someday. A license was never the goal. What would I have done with it anyway? There were no female pilots. My role models had not yet appeared on the scene. The airline professionals and their peers had convinced me that their career was not an option. And yet, here I was.

I explained that all the hours in the logbook were spent learning and practicing maneuvers and landings. However, with no navigation or communication radios, flaps, lights, or wheels on the Cub, it was impossible to perform the requirements for a license. I pointed out that I got my licenses and ratings more quickly after switching to a landplane because the extra flight hours went toward the higher time totals required.

The panel of recruiters generally sat together on one side of a table across from the interviewee. I tried to make eye contact with everyone, not talk too much with my hands or ramble, which I tend to do when I'm nervous. (I quickly learned not to wear silk blouses to the interviews because they easily show sweat.)

The pilot recruiters spent a lot of time thumbing through my logbook, which read like a diary, detailing the lessons of the day. The question of how I paid for all the extra hours of lessons came up with the implication that the exchange must have included something other than gas money. I was used to such innuendos, but it surprised me in an interview's formal, professional setting.

I usually connected best with the HR guy, who seemed to enjoy having a civilian in the interview chair for a change. He smiled the most and made comments to make me more comfortable. I hoped my honesty and sincerity made up for my unusual background.

At the start of one airline's interview, it was apparent that I had taken them by surprise. "Oh, well, I guess Lynn could be a girl's name as well," someone said. There was no box to check for gender since only one was allowed. I wondered whether I would have been called in if they knew this Lynn was female.

There were always questions about in-flight emergency procedures, for which I prepared. However, they knew nothing about the Twin Otter, so I wondered if my preparation even mattered. One interview got very strange when they asked how I would respond if the captain were incapacitated. The obvious answer to me was to continue flying the plane from the right seat, which was an option on all the aircraft I knew. They persisted in asking again to see if that was my final answer, asking if I didn't want to remove him from the seat. I wondered if they were just having fun at my expense, making a point that I wasn't strong enough to accomplish that or seeing if they could rattle me enough to change my mind to appease them. I wanted to say, "Do you ask your male candidates this question?" but was afraid of appearing combative. I left not knowing the correct answer or their intent—and still don't.

Another strange exchange had to do with my being a flight attendant. They questioned if I thought being a flight attendant was a means to becoming a pilot and if I were going to encourage other flight attendants to apply. The thought made them visibly uneasy. One pilot even tried to talk me out of continuing with the interview process. According to him, I had so many other more attractive and appropriate options—for a girl.

"You're still employed as a TWA flight attendant with six years of seniority and excellent work history. Are you sure you want to give that up? Your major and experience are in teaching and psychology—not quite subjects for a future pilot, are they? Isn't teaching an excellent career for a woman? Why leave it?"

If they looked carefully at the timeline, they could see I graduated from college *after* starting work as a flight attendant. The butterfly leave that allowed me to train and work as a pilot in Miami while also working as a flight attendant based in New York was baffling to some. I was accused of not being fully committed to my new path as a pilot because I was still employed as a flight attendant. Most interviews ended with the question of what I would do if I weren't selected, for which I had a ready, honest answer.

"I'll continue applying to other airlines until I am hired. I'm more qualified than many; I know I would do the job well and be a good employee. I have other interviews scheduled, but I would prefer not to need to go to those."

The physical exam was always the last step. The male clinic technicians were as unused to dealing with a female applicant as the interviewers. Taking a chest x-ray and EKG of someone with breasts was an uncommon and uncomfortable event for the poor guys.

Usually, applicants who made it to the physical were next to be hired unless there was a medical problem. I was very healthy, so I was excited to make it to this final stage at Ozark and American. However, after the exams, I came up short at both airlines—in inches. American told me they had a minimum height requirement of 5 feet, 6 inches. At 5 feet, 4 inches, I was deemed too short to fly. Figuring I had nothing to lose, I protested, arguing that I had seen American male pilots as short as I am in the terminal, that the seats were adjustable, and that I knew for a fact that I could reach all the switches and controls. The recruiter wasn't expecting an argument. The best response he could offer was, "Well, we're looking for a uniform look here, so that's the minimum."

Ozark, with their 5 feet, 5 inches minimum, also found me unacceptable. A flight attendant friend in law school urged me to sue, saying I could win a case on discrimination. I worried about the reception I would receive after being hired under protest and decided to consider it their loss. Besides, I was still awaiting a call from my number one choice, TWA.

It finally arrived. The invitation to interview as a TWA B-727 flight engineer came in the mail. My sources had assured me that TWA did not have the same arbitrary height requirement that sent me home from American and Ozark. Instead, they would want to see that I could reach all of the switches and controls in the cockpit from either seat and pass a first officer flight check in the B-707, which seemed fair. I didn't mind at all. A pilot friend in the training department had let me fly the simulator before, probably to see for himself if I was capable. It was great fun to prove that even a girl could fly a jet.

The TWA interview didn't go as smoothly as I had hoped. I was sure I looked nervous and impatient at times with their lack of knowledge and understanding of my situation. They hadn't heard of the butterfly leave and knew nothing of the Twin Otter or turboprops. They were hardly aware of a civilian path to a major airline career, and of course, they knew nothing about a woman's path to it.

On the flight home from the interview and over the following days, the interview questions replayed over and over in my head as I rephrased my answers in a futile attempt at a redo. Had I talked too much, sounded too "girly," shown too much emotion, and ended up doing more harm than good in advancing women in aviation? Perhaps they had decided "no" before I even walked in and were just having fun filling the time slot. I would counter myself with my own argument that it must have gone reasonably well, or they wouldn't have sent me on to the physical.

To keep from going crazy, figuring I had nothing to lose, I wrote a letter to the recruiting department, re-answering their questions with more candid and concise explanations. I ended with my sincere reasons for wanting to continue working with my TWA family and aviation home—now as a pilot.

I hoped the HR representative sitting with the two pilots at the interview table carried weight in the decision since he seemed to be my strongest ally. I have no idea how that discussion went, if anyone read my letter, or whether it made a difference, until a month later when a reply finally arrived.

"Congratulations, you have been…"

I DID IT! I had a job offer to be an airline pilot—a TWA pilot! My dream, a very long-standing dream, had come true.

I was moving to the other side of the cockpit door—to fly the planes where I had served meals!

Last trip as TWA Flight Attendant 1978

20

The Girls Are Okay

I showed my acceptance letter to my TWA flight attendant supervisor, who had helped me along the way and was thrilled for our success. I flew my last trip as a flight attendant and received a departmental transfer to pilot—from cabin to cockpit—the first in history to make such a move.

In November 1978, I arrived at the pilot training center in Kansas City for a B-727 flight engineer training class, the steppingstone to the front-row seat as a first officer and eventually captain. Classrooms and simulators filled the pilot training center with state-of-the-art teaching aids showing the airplane's systems in visual displays of primary-colored lights. An overhead projector used multiple overlays to illustrate the flow of the electrical, hydraulic, fuel, pneumatic, and air-conditioning systems throughout the plane. As flight engineers, our responsibility was monitoring and controlling these systems from our panel to keep the plane and its occupants alive and comfortable.

TWA, as well as most other major airlines at the time, were flying Boeing's most popular creation, the 727. With its three engines mounted aft, near the tail, the interior noise was much less in the cabin and cockpit, earning her the moniker "the Whisperjet" at some airlines. Depending on the plane's configuration, it could carry one-hundred forty-eight to two-hundred eighty-nine passengers. And while it could fly as fast as six hundred miles per hour at altitudes up to forty thousand feet, commercial airlines went lower and slower for passenger comfort and fuel economy.

I had learned much of the study material in Mr. Archibald's class, but now the goal was more than helping the guys pass a test or getting a good grade and a certificate I thought I could never use. Now it was about my job. I would be responsible for the comfort and safety of passengers. I was motivated to study as I had never been motivated before.

TWA had not had a training class in eight years, so all the instructors seemed genuinely glad to see new blood joining the ranks, making the training building come alive again. I was one of three female trainees in the first two classes. Karen Davies, TWA's first female pilot, was followed by Terrie Foote and me just two weeks later. The three of us quickly became fast friends despite our different personalities and backgrounds. Our shared goals, the yearning for camaraderie, and a wish to survive and succeed far outweighed any minor personal disparities.

Karen grew up in an aviation family with a father who was a TWA pilot. She wanted to follow in his footsteps and make him proud. A strong woman with short brown hair, she entertained her interviewers by saying she "put her pants on one leg at a time just like everyone else." She had an easy, confident way of being one of the guys that I envied. Extremely competent, blunt, and straightforward in her communication, it was helpful having her in the class ahead to give us a peek at what was coming next.

Terrie was as far opposite from Karen as I could imagine. Hailing from North Carolina, where she had briefly flown for Piedmont Airlines, she was a true Southern belle. Naturally curly, long, light brown hair framed her face with its smooth, fair complexion, long lashes, and white teeth. She was tall and slender with a sweet Southern drawl that transfixed men, causing them to offer to help before she even asked. Unlike me, trying to prove myself in a man's world through stubborn independence, she saw nothing wrong with accepting offers to carry her bags and crew kit. Her wedding ring allowed the casual flirting without the complications I didn't dare risk. Terrie also had a brilliant mind, remarkable memory, and sweet disposition. She became a wonderful friend and classmate.

Although I don't remember any of us saying it out loud, we knew we held the hope and future of female pilots in our hands. Whatever one of us did immediately spread through the ranks as a story about "one of the girls." It was apparent that each of us was responsible for the reputation and image of our individual selves, but also universally—for one another and those who would follow. We quickly learned we needed to be the best to be accepted as okay and to be extraordinary to be considered average. We were assumed unable to understand technical (manly) information until we proved otherwise.

Our male classmates, also in their late twenties, quickly became allies and a strong support system as we helped one another study, memorize, review, and prepare for the unending quizzes and exams that filled our days. Terrie and I took on the role of social coordinator, inviting everyone to study sessions to compare notes taken in class that day, pool our knowledge, and help one another succeed. Sometimes, Karen or the guys in the class ahead would join in. We joked that absorbing all the information coming at us was like drinking from a fire hose.

During our first week of training, we were asked to show our ability to fly the simulator from the right seat, where we would sit when we eventually upgraded to first officer. Our instructor explained why this extra step had been added. Seven years earlier, a pilot shortage caused by the Vietnam War prompted a radical experiment called the zero-time pilot program. Pilot applicants were only required to have a commercial license, instrument rating, and a college degree in anything. The theory was that brains were more important than hours of experience, which could always be acquired.

Once hired, TWA supplied the training to be a flight engineer, but that was all. Since the flight engineer position didn't require any time at the controls of the plane, this had worked great for a while. TWA's natural expectation was that the grateful new-hires would continue flying lessons on their own to prepare to upgrade to the first officer seat, a flying position. However, many of the new engineers felt that if TWA wanted them to keep flying, TWA should pay for it. So, they did nothing. Seven years later, when attrition demanded they upgrade, they could not pass the flight test to be a first officer. TWA had an up-or-out policy, meaning if a pilot couldn't progress in the expected manner from flight engineer to first officer to captain, they were fired. It was no surprise that some were washing out, losing their jobs, wasting the time and expense of training, and adding to the present pilot demand. TWA wanted to make sure we women didn't create the same problem in the future, even though our hiring requirements and interview had been much more stringent.

We heard rumors that we had been hired with the plan to wash us out during training. It would prove once and for all piloting commercial airplanes was no career for a woman. I knew rumors were always rampant at an airline and figured it was just some guy's wish he chose to verbalize. We knew better than to believe it, but still, it weighed on us.

It didn't help when I entered the elevator in the training center with the VP of training one day. Called "The Dark Knight," his nickname reflected his disposition and reputation in the training center. I started to tell him how pleased I was to have been hired when he cut me off with, "We don't hire women." I wondered if he hadn't heard me correctly, was in denial, or if no one had the guts to tell him his airline had, indeed, hired three women. Or was it his way of telling me we weren't long for this program, and per the rumor, they would soon be back to normal, pretending we never happened?

Fortunately, there were also many good guys, our angels, who wanted us to succeed. They wanted their daughters to have career options. Others just thought it right for us to have the same opportunities and support that their male peers enjoyed. Most importantly, these fellow pilots helped spread the word: "The girls are okay."

TWA B-727 Flight Engineer January, 1979

At the flight engineer's panel

21

Trials, Tears, and Tenacity

After training, we had a month to move to our New York LaGuardia base before reporting for our IOE, initial operating experience, the final step before officially taking the role of TWA pilots. Karen, Terrie, and I agreed we wanted—no, *needed*—to room together to stay sane in the world we were entering. Karen graduated first, so we entrusted her with finding us a home.

Karen found a house in Long Beach, a few blocks from where I lived as a flight attendant and affordable with our probationary salary. Although my annual pay had doubled from Air Illinois, it was only $12,000 until our second year, when it would double again. The "big bucks" everyone thought pilots made would be far in the future and only for a select few. No one I knew entered a piloting career for the money. The job held too many uncertainties, changes, and unexpected events out of one's control. It took someone with a high "chaos quotient," a sense of adventure, and a true love for aviation. Hopefully, that described TWA's first three female pilots.

One of the first visitors to our home was Angus from PR briefing us on our role in the public's eye. Angus was very pleased to have us as a diversion to take the public's attention away from a recent TWA aircraft incident. In mid-flight, a 727 spiraled out of control over Michigan, dropping over 30,000 feet in a few minutes before recovering and making an emergency landing at Detroit Metropolitan Airport. The captain was proclaimed a hero when, in fact, the National Transportation Safety Board determined he and the flight crew under his command had caused the problem.

Angus told us what had happened. The 727's wing has movable parts called flaps behind the wing and leading-edge devices in front that are designed to move together with the placement of a single lever in the cockpit. They extend to increase lift at slower speeds for takeoff and landing. They are supposed to stay retracted in flight. Only by pulling a circuit breaker can one part be moved without the other. Pilots trying to save gas had theorized and discovered that extending the flaps just one degree without the leading edges did, in fact, cause the plane to fly flatter. To decrease drag and therefore use less fuel, they would pull the leading-edge circuit breaker to deactivate them and then move the flap lever to extend only the one degree of trailing edge flaps. Of course, this was not sanctioned by the airline nor the FAA.

The captain, in this case, liked to use this trick. While the flight engineer was in the bathroom, the captain pulled the circuit breaker and extended the flaps one degree. Upon his return, the flight engineer did what any flight engineer seeing a popped circuit breaker would do and pushed it back in. The leading-edge devices began to extend, but not equally or simultaneously. The plane violently tipped from one side to the other and suddenly dropped thousands of feet due to the additional and uneven drag. The captain wrestled to get it under control, slowed, corrected the problem by retracting the flaps and leading-edge devices, and got the damaged plane on the ground.

Upon landing, the passengers hailed him a hero, and he didn't correct them. In fact, in the newspaper reports, he credited his years as an aerobatic pilot for saving all their lives.

Angus was concerned if the press went looking into the "hero's" past, they would find numerous DWI arrests, including one for driving a hundred miles an hour on the LA freeway and another for driving erratically on a motorcycle.

Angus needed a PR diversion, and he planned to show us off. He sent me to make a presentation at the St. Louis airport, Lindbergh Field, near my hometown where I was photographed with the mayor. I was concerned at first that our male counterparts would resent the added attention and PR gigs we were getting, but I found no hard feelings at all. I understood why. Like most of them, I also felt much more comfortable in the cockpit than in front of people and cameras.

We three were hoping for a smooth transition from training to the flight line, but we were realistic. The men's outcry in opposition to females in their workplace started while we were in training. When some complained that they should be allowed the same dress code, we women had to dress like men: hair above the collar and ears, no earrings or makeup, no tailoring of the uniform or accessories to feminize it. We were to wear the same belted black slacks, white shirt, black tie, and boxy suit they wore. When I went to have my uniform fitting, the very nice tailor took my measurements and then complained to his coworker. "She's a perfect size 5. How can I cut even the smallest uniform down to that?"

And the hat didn't help. I hated it. The one-size-fits-all large circular top, with headband adjusted to my small head, looked like a flying saucer had landed there. Evidently, my dislike for the hat was shared by many, as there was a hat clip attachment for the flight bag that allowed the pilot to comply with the requirement to "have the hat on your person at all times" without actually wearing it.

It was interesting and somewhat frustrating to find that my female peers at American Airlines told a completely different story. A college degree wasn't initially required, and they didn't need jet time, or high flight time to apply. Once hired, they were allowed to help design their tailored uniform and hat, got makeup and packing-for-layovers advice, and enjoyed a welcoming environment. It resulted in a completely different experience for them and their airline.

Although most flight engineers had the training and certificates to fly the jet, the role did not include touching the yoke. Instead, my responsibilities included first performing the walkaround, a visual inspection of the plane's exterior to ensure all the parts and pieces were in place and there were no leaks. Brakes, tires, fluids, emergency oxygen, and fire-retardant levels all had to be within limits. Onboard the plane, I monitored the systems—electrical, fuel, hydraulic, pneumatic, pressurization, cabin temperature, and oxygen—and dealt with any system abnormalities or emergencies. I was responsible for adjusting the throttles and monitoring the engines while helping with the radio calls, making passenger announcements, and providing a third set of eyes. Being closest to the cockpit door, getting coffee was often added to the flight engineer's duties. The guys didn't seem to mind having a woman in that seat get the coffee, but some reassigned the duty of making passenger announcements, citing concern that passengers would find a feminine voice from the cockpit unsettling.

My hand reaching forward to adjust the throttles also triggered comments about my bracelet, rings, or fingernail polish being "just not right" or "disturbing and distracting." After complying with all the uniform rules, my attire was still under scrutiny, so I dropped even those small tokens of femininity. The message was clear: If you want to be in a man's world, you will look and act like one as much as possible.

The flight engineer's desk stored the logbook, maintenance records, and pay cards, as well as the *Playboy* centerfold of the month. I knew pin-up calendars and girly magazines were common in male-dominated enclaves such as frat houses, garages, and bars. The cockpit was no different. The "artwork" was out of public view, but everywhere—inside the logbook cover, taped to the inside and underside of the desk, inside the emergency rope and oxygen mask compartments, the yoke cap, and any panel marked with an "X." Removing the panel with a screwdriver rewarded the seeker with a visual treat. I could never understand this form of male pleasure, but I accepted it as one of the gender differences and ignored it. The intention was not personal, so it seemed easy to overlook and accept as part of the all-male world I had entered.

On our first several flights, an in-flight instructor went along to give on-the-job training and explain the real-world procedures. The instructor pointed out the differences from the ivory-tower information given by classroom instructors who "just teach it but don't do it." When any of us three women had an experience or found a kind soul willing to teach these secrets, we brought the information home to share. The in-flight instructors watched our every move and ultimately gave us their blessing. They seemed unexpectedly pleased with our level of knowledge and ability.

I was uncertain of the welcome I would receive from the pilots I used to serve but was now joining as an equal. Many had helped me study along the way and encouraged me to go as far as I could, but none expected me to actually make it as far as they had. I was also uncertain of the reaction waiting from my flight attendant friends who may feel I was abandoning them or thought that I felt I was now superior to them.

When I saw my TWA peers after training was completed, I was pleasantly surprised and relieved to find all my flight attendant friends were proud and supportive. They were thrilled for me, especially the males. They explained that it opened doors for everyone, breaking down gender-specific roles and expectations. Having a woman in the cockpit made it easier for a man to work in the cabin. Many of them knew how hard I had worked to become a pilot and liked having someone up front who could relate to what was going on in the back. A few were even inspired to start taking flying lessons themselves.

Out on the flight line, every trip was to a different city with a new crew who needed to see for themselves what we were made of. A rumor had spread claiming women were hired with different, lesser qualifications, which was true of some airlines that had implemented quotas, but not TWA. On each trip, we were assumed incompetent until tested and proven otherwise. It was demeaning and frustrating and got old fast. Everything we did was lumped together as news about "the girls."

As new hires and the most junior on the seniority list, we were on reserve, which meant we had to be no more than an hour's drive to either of the New York airports. Although most of our 727 flights departed from and returned to LaGuardia, leaving from JFK was also a possibility. With a reserve schedule, we were given ten days off that could be grouped into one, two, or three blocks of time. During our days on duty, we could be assigned to flights going anywhere at any time, so a clean uniform, a packed bag, and a crew kit with up-to-date manuals always had to be ready. Fortunately, we were good at our jobs, blessed with social and coping skills, patience, and a sense of humor—critical traits for our sanity and survival. No matter how bad the trip, we three housemates knew we could return home to relay the latest events to another who truly understood what it was like out there.

In addition to the stories, we shared the never-ending complaints from our fellow pilots:

Now they couldn't burp, fart, curse, or pee into a bottle freely.

We made the work environment uncomfortable and therefore unsafe.

We were a distraction.

They would have to do their jobs *and* ours.

It wasn't natural or the correct order of things.

It was against God's plan (accompanied by Bible quotes).

We were taking jobs from men who needed to provide for families, taking food from the mouths of children.

It was a waste of the airline's training slots and money since we would just get married and/or pregnant and quit.

Or, worse yet, *not* get married or pregnant and not quit, but expect to become a captain. That would be *really* unsafe because no man in his right mind could /would /should be expected to take orders from a woman.

So, in short, we were selfishly messing it up for everyone.

Some of the pilots who knew me from my flight attendant days approached me as a friend to try to help me understand and talk some sense into me.

"You're such a nice person and a wonderful flight attendant. Why are you causing all this trouble?"

"I'm sure you were a good flight instructor. Women are such natural teachers. Wouldn't you rather do that?"

"Don't you think you would have a better chance of finding a husband while working as a flight attendant rather than a pilot?"

"Aren't you afraid people will think you're gay?"

"What are you trying to prove?"

I tried to help them understand by saying, "Wouldn't you want your daughter or wife to have all the career options possible?"

"Oh, I would never let my wife do something like this!" was the inevitable reply.

I thought how strange the words "let my wife" sounded to me.

I got used to the pornography hidden throughout the cockpit and the common topics of male conversations. I took none of it personally and figured it was part of entering a man's world. Sometimes, however, even patience and a sense of humor weren't enough to get me through without tears.

On one flight, after we leveled off at altitude and turned on the autopilot, both pilots lit cigars and began puffing away, filling the cockpit with thick, stinky smoke. When I couldn't take it anymore, I tried to be tactful.

"Hey, guys, my dad smokes cigars, too, but in a truck with the windows open. We can't open these windows. Can you please stop?"

They looked at each other, smiling, and both reached for something I could see they had placed there in anticipation of the moment. "We thought you might say that. Why don't you just join us? Here's one of your brand."

Tampons.

They each tried to hand me a tampon.

I fell back in my seat to get as far away as possible in the confined space. I wanted to leave, get away from them, get away from it all. I was too embarrassed and shocked to say anything—and they were loving it. For the rest of the flight, I said nothing other than the required responses. But it wasn't over. They were waiting for me in the dispatch area, where I had to go with the post-flight paperwork.

"Hey, we were wondering if you could give us a lift to the crew hotel. You have a car, right? We both commute and don't want to wait for the hotel bus."

I was shaking and close to tears, but I finally found my voice.

"After that, you want a *favor?*"

They took turns with their comebacks and advice.

"Hey, we're the good guys just trying to get you ready for what's out there."

"That was nothing. Have a sense of humor."

"You want to fit in, right? Well, laugh at yourself and with us."

"Don't be so sensitive."

"That was funny; I don't care who you are."

And the finale:

"If you can't stand the heat, get back in the kitchen."

I did give them a ride because that's how I am and how the world worked if I wanted the job. The jerks chatted casually in the back seat while I drove in silence to the motel, angry at myself for not being more assertive, not saying "enough" or "no." I had seen it before and wondered why bullies often added the extra insult of asking a favor of the victim. If the victim complies, the abuse must be acceptable and no big deal. If the favor is denied, the victim is the bad guy. Quite a trick.

After dropping them off in silence, I made it all the way home before I finally broke into tears in my car. Inside the house, I sank into the easy chair and announced to my roommates, "I don't know if I can take anymore." At some point, each of us had come home with something that pushed us to the limit. We were glad to have a place to unload and vent, be supported and encouraged to continue, and not let them win. It felt like a battle at times and very lonely.

Not all our peers acted so crudely. Going through the demanding training experience created a tight group among those in our classes who stayed in touch. Gradually, an increasing number of pilots were also willing to make us feel welcome, offer assistance, come to our defense when needed, and make life in the cockpit more bearable.

Sadly, some women at other airlines didn't have the support we finally received. They suffered ongoing harassment that caused severe depression, which, in turn, caused poor performance. The familiar phrase those bully pilots had used, "If you can't stand the heat, get back in the kitchen," seemed to be a favorite and even spread to the guys in air traffic control, radar rooms, and the tower talking to planes over the radio. When a feminine voice responded to a radio call, a male voice on the frequency would often say, "There goes another empty kitchen," or "Get back in the kitchen."

Sometimes, it was even cruder. As a new 737 arrived in Houston with a female voice calling for landing clearance, a male response was heard.

"Brand new airplane and already got a crack in it."

Responding in kind only escalated the situation, and we women were sorely outnumbered. At less than one percent, the odds were not in our favor.

It wasn't just our aviation coworkers who reacted to our presence. Passengers were surprised and seemed ready to accept any explanation other than "lady pilot," two words some couldn't imagine together, an oxymoron.

"Oh, look, the pilots have a secretary now."

"Isn't that cute? The captain brought his daughter dressed up just like him."

"Why did that one flight attendant stay up in the cockpit the whole flight?"

"Does she get paid more for working up there?"

"Is she one of the pilots' girlfriends? Is that a good idea to have her up there?"

"She doesn't touch anything, right?"

Or the captain would take it upon himself to offer, "Don't worry, we won't let her do anything but sit there and look pretty." Followed by laughter, of course.

Even in my hometown, acceptance of my new position was unsettling for some. The editor of the local paper approached me to say, "Your mom tells me TWA hired you as a pilot, but they don't let you fly the plane, right?" Because I was still a flight engineer, I affirmed the remark and then tried to explain the seniority and upgrade system that would allow me to fly one day, but he had the answer he needed to be comfortable and walked away.

Soon after our arrival on the scene, the pilots' union rep contacted us and wanted to know what we expected the union to do. Taken by surprise, we asked what he meant.

"Pregnancy! Now that you are here, we have to come up with a policy for when you get pregnant. So, what do you expect the union to do?"

The man on the phone sounded irritated at saying the word, much less dealing with such an unsavory subject and its cause—us.

We considered telling them not to worry. None of us planned on being pregnant anytime soon, but then we realized we needed to get something in the contract for the future and other women. As the English major, I was appointed to submit our proposal.

I knew of no other airlines with pregnant pilot policies, so I looked to the flight attendants' contract. They were required to report their condition to their supervisor and go on maternity leave immediately. Just a few years prior to that, having a thirty-fourth birthday or pregnancy led to dismissal. At one time, marriage ended a flight attendant's career. In early aviation history, a pilot lost her medical certificate and pilot license when pregnant and had to reapply for both all over again after the birth. We had come a long way, but still had a long road ahead as women in aviation.

I wanted to suggest something ground-breaking, reflective of the new era. I thought it should be similar to the flight attendants' policy but also fair and representative of men. So, I suggested that women be allowed time off on medical leave for the months of pregnancy plus an additional three months off after giving birth. To be fair, I added that fathers could also apply for "paternity leave," allowing them time at home after the baby's birth (or adoption). Soon after we sent in the proposal, the union rep called again, even more irate than before.

"Are you trying to get me laughed off the council? What's this crap about paternity leave? No real man in his right mind stays home to take care of a baby. That's what the mom is for. Who in the hell would want to take time off then? We sign up for extra trips to be gone more. And you want a *year* off to have a baby—WITH PAY?! I tell you girls right now—the day one of you takes time off for a planned medical—because that's exactly what becoming pregnant is—an on-purpose, planned medical— that's when I go fishing and expect to be paid for it! You send me something sensible. This is no joke."

He hung up before I could respond.

I copied what was in the flight attendant manual and sent it to him, thinking if the company had already agreed to it there, it would work for us as pilots for now. We would have to wage one battle at a time.

I had another battle, a more personal one, waiting for me in Miami. Sam and I celebrated my new job, but it was bittersweet. We had struggled through the separation that Air Illinois had created. Theoretically, we could use passes to fly to see the other, but we were so busy at our respective airlines "building hours" that being together became a lesser priority. I felt our relationship was strong enough to see us through the time apart, but there was another concern.

I had the job Sam had been dreaming of his whole life. With his father and older brother flying for TWA, he desperately wanted to join them—but not badly enough to return to school for the required four-year degree. There was nothing more to discuss, but the unaddressed issue became a no-fly zone between us. Since Sam hated New York, I promised to go to Miami as often as possible.

TWA Pilots 40 years later. Retired Pilot Reunion 2019

22

Welcome Lady Pilots

My reserve schedule gave me blocks of free time, allowing me to return to the Miami apartment and Sam. Running errands one day, I passed a motel sign with the greeting, "Welcome Lady Pilots." I turned around at the next light to make sure I had read it correctly. "Lady Pilots?" Were there enough of us to create a gathering? I had to go inside to find out more.

The gentleman at the front desk assured me there was indeed "a whole bunch of 'em out by the pool," as he pointed me in the right direction. A group of swimsuit-clad women in their twenties lounged in and beside the pool, animated in conversation and enjoying the sun, water, and one another's company. I approached the nearest one to find out more.

"Hi. Excuse me, but I understand you are all airline pilots?"

"Yes. Yes, we are," she replied with a smile and evident pride. Then a bit more hesitantly. "Why do you ask?"

"I am too—a pilot that is—for TWA. I saw the sign out front, and—" My explanation was cut short.

"Hey, everybody. Here's TWA!" she shouted above the chatter.

One by one, they made their way over to greet me, introduced themselves, and invited me to join in. I could hardly believe it and couldn't wait to tell Karen and Terrie. There were more of us! Evidently, the airlines weren't advertising the fact.

Almost every airline was represented with at least one female pilot – Denise from U.S. Air; Jean and Gail from United; Lennie, Claudia, and Karen from Continental; and Terry at Western. I got to meet Emily Howell, the Frontier pilot, and thank her in person for her letter encouraging me to pursue a career as a pilot—it worked! They explained that some of the first women hired by various airlines knew of each other and came up with the idea for a social organization of women pilots. Feeling the need for a support system, in May 1978, they invited women from all the airlines to meet in Las Vegas. Twenty-one accepted the invitation. Each was one of the first women at their airline. International Social Affiliation of Women Airline Pilots, or ISA+21, was born from their desire for an aviatrix sisterhood.

The name was an attempt to use the initials for International Standard Atmosphere, which in aviation provides a standard for the atmosphere's temperature, density, and pressure. The +21 is to honor the twenty-one women who responded to the invitation and became the charter members. ISA+21 is quite a deviation from the standard or norm, which was an apt description of women in aviation. The name was soon changed to International Society of Women Airline Pilots.

The women who gathered in Miami that day in May 1979 gave me new hope and encouragement for the future of our gender in the airlines. They were young, bright, and interesting. They loved flying and their careers. Each had a fascinating story of why they started flying and how they ended up at their airline. Many had fathers in aviation or, in Terry London Rinehart's case, a mother who was a WASP (Women Airforce Service Pilots) in WWII. Others lived near small airports and initially fell in love with flying as a sport or hobby as I did. Some were married, but most were single. They told of varying degrees of acceptance at the different airlines and among their male co-workers. There would be no shortage of topics of conversation with this group. I was thrilled to be invited to join them the next day. Before parting, we exchanged contact information and promises to stay in touch. These women were facing the same challenges and looking for solutions just like me. We could share experiences and advice, provide a network of support.

I attended ISA conventions the following years in Denver, Cancun, and Jamaica and served as secretary for two years. One of the organization's purposes was to promote and support other young women wanting to be commercial pilots. Remembering what a difference Richard Bach's encouragement, belief in me, and monetary support made in my life, I volunteered to be on the scholarship committee. I wanted to do all I could to help other young women know about career opportunities available in aviation and help them achieve their goals. It has remained an ongoing effort throughout my life.

At one of our conventions, I offered to fill a lull in the action with an event that I thought everyone would find relevant and humorous, my favorite female pilot story.

Flights had been canceled and delayed all day while we waited for the weather to improve so we could return to New York from Miami. Finally, as dusk approached, our TWA 727 was among a long line of planes taxiing to the active runway. Just when it was our turn to go, tower announced that due to airspace saturation (too many planes in too little space), there would be another one-hour delay before takeoff. We pulled over to the side of the run-up area and shut down engines to save fuel. The long line of planes behind us did the same.

The captain relayed the disappointing news to the passengers and told the flight attendants to serve the meals and offer everyone free drinks. Within a few moments, the senior flight attendant came up to the cockpit.

"Captain, we have a problem," she said. "One of the passengers has a seeing-eye dog. After waiting so long in the terminal and now on the plane, the dog has to go to the bathroom."

After myriad bathroom jokes and ridiculous solutions, the other pilots concluded the canine plumbing problem fell to the "plumber," a nickname for the flight engineer. I thought for a moment and then realized I *did* have an answer. The 727 has aft stairs under the tail that can be lowered from the cockpit. With engines shut down, jet blast wouldn't be a problem. I suggested to the captain that we lower the stairs to allow the dog to do his thing in the grass by the tarmac. He agreed and called tower to get permission to take a dog for a much-needed walk. They found it amusing but said okay, so I lowered the stairs.

I told the flight attendant our good idea. She was pleased but very busy.

"Lynn, I have to help give all of these people meals and drinks. Could you talk to the lady?"

Sure, I thought. I'm not busy. I found the owner of the dog and told her the good news. She could take the dog outside to the grass.

"Honey, I can't do that. I'm blind," she said, stating the obvious. And then, with a sweet smile, "But I'll tell him it's okay to go with you."

I couldn't back out now and truly did want to help, so I got my uniform coat and hat from the cockpit, took the dog by his harness, and proceeded down the aisle and down the stairs. When the dog saw the answer to his prayers, he couldn't wait to get to the grass. He ran, pulling me along right onto the grass with him— where I sank knee-deep in Florida mud. The rain had turned the ground into a quagmire. When I pulled my foot out of the hole, my shoe didn't come with it. With the dog doing his thing, I was down on my hands and knees, groping for my shoe in the black sludge. Just then, a gust of wind came along to lift off my uniform hat, rolling it like a Frisbee across the cement. With dripping shoe in one hand, dog harness in the other, I limped off after my runaway hat. I was so glad that it was almost dark, and no one could see what was happening.

Suddenly, Delta, who was parked behind us, turned on their wing lights, lighting up my entire world like floodlights on a stage. Terrific. Now everyone could see what was happening. Limping, I hurried the best I could to get back to the plane. Wet and muddy, with hat and shoe in one hand and a much happier seeing-eye dog in the other, I climbed the stairs and delivered the dog to one of the flight attendants so that I could clean up in the aft lavatory. When I returned to the cockpit, the captain and first officer were laughing so hard they could hardly speak. Wiping tears from their eyes, they told the story.

After the pilots in the Delta plane turned on the spotlights, they spoke on tower frequency monitored by all the planes that had watched the show.

"Hey, TWA. We know this anti-discrimination thing is the latest rage, but don't you think hiring a blind, lame female is taking it a bit too far?"

One ISA member in the audience liked the story so much she submitted it to *Reader's Digest*'s "Laughter is the Best Medicine" and received a fifty-dollar reward for sharing my most embarrassing moment.

ISA 1979

ISA convention 1980

23

Two Loves

Nearing our one-year anniversary as TWA flight engineers, my roommates and I were enjoying our new work schedules and environment. We were no longer on reserve and were beginning to feel accepted by our peers. Then, two weeks shy of completing our probationary period and doubling our meager paychecks, we got the news.

We were furloughed, the airline's term for laid off due to over-staffing.

The aviation industry is notorious for being extremely volatile, frantically hiring or conducting massive layoffs, sometimes both simultaneously as departments miscommunicate. Flying is not a career for those needing assurance and stability. Since my biggest fear when contemplating a future was boredom, I figured I got what I asked for.

I had lived through the upheaval of a furlough before as a flight attendant and decided the time off might again have a silver lining. Sam, who was still living and flying in Miami, had given me an engagement ring. The furlough would allow us to share more time together as we became a significant part of each other's lives. During the year of my flying at Air Illinois, followed by TWA training in Kansas City, and being based in New York, we had been separated more than we would have liked. The furlough would let us make up for the time apart.

I took Sam to Vermont and showed him where my flying began. Ted gave us his blessing, and Bill made an exception to his girls-only rule and took Sam for a ride in the seaplane. We visited my family in Illinois and his in the Bahamas. Everyone seemed to get along well and was happy for us.

Roommate Karen came home with the exciting news that a JFK-based cargo airline called Seaboard World Airlines was hiring pilots. They flew DC-8s, a four-engine jet based in London, England, and the newer, larger 747, flew from JFK, New York. She had already applied and suggested Terrie and I do the same. We both declined, preferring to spend the unexpected three-month hiatus with our special someones.

I told Sam about the opportunity. With his prior Miami cargo-flying experience, I thought he would have a good chance at the job. If he were based in New York, we would have more time together. A warm-weather, beach-loving guy to the core, he was not excited about New York, but the opportunity to fly a large jet was enticing enough for him to fly up for the interview.

The Seaboard World cargo building was on a part of the JFK airport I had never seen. It seemed strange to drive my car onto the cargo ramp and park next to a hangar filled with planes. I planned to wait in the car while Sam went inside a door labeled "office" to find the chief pilot. I had brought a book along to read but couldn't stop looking at the gorgeous 747 sitting on the ramp right outside my car window. The paint job was an elegant gold and black with a large white stripe bearing the name Seaboard World Containership covering the entire side, unobstructed by the windows of a passenger plane. The only windows on this plane were three stories up, on the "hump," the highest level, where the cockpit was located. The nose cone, just below the cockpit, was hinged on the top and open. I watched huge forklifts place metal containers the size of train cars inside. They were loading the space that would have held almost four hundred passengers on my TWA planes and still had the cargo space below to fill through the side belly doors.

Despite her size, the 747 appeared the most graceful when she was on approach for landing. They said it was an optical illusion due to her size and relatively low speed, but she seemed to float, flying in slow motion over the runway threshold. The landings were the best, too, with all eighteen tires to distribute the weight touching down in turn. It seemed incredible that someone had dreamt it, drew it, and made that plane a reality. The 747 was the largest commercial airplane in the world, boasting the most advanced technology and aircraft systems. The 747-200 cargo version could weigh over 880,000 pounds fully loaded, while the more common passenger version had a seating capacity of up to four hundred. With four powerful engines, the plane had a cruise speed of five hundred miles per hour, a range of seven thousand eight hundred miles, and a service ceiling of forty-five thousand feet. The fuselage was more than twice the size of any other plane. At two-hundred-thirty feet long and a wingspan of two-hundred feet, if placed on a football field, the 747 would be only twenty yards shy of taking up the entire space! The tail rose above the four-story building next to me. The engine nacelles were so big I could stand inside with arms outstretched and not touch the sides.

All the TWA pilots I knew looked forward to the day they would be senior enough to fly the Queen of the Skies.

I was still waiting in the car when the sun went down, and I was getting cold. I decided to venture inside for warmth. Inside the metal door was a dimly lit, narrow hallway and no one in sight. I poked my head in the first open door and saw a middle-aged woman sitting at a desk filled with papers. She looked up, surprised, but spoke pleasantly.

"Yes? May I help you?"

"Sorry to startle you. I'm waiting for Sam. I think he's here in an interview."

"Of course. Come on in and have a seat. I can't leave until the boss does, so you can wait here. I'm Alice." She smiled and seemed glad to have the company.

"I'm Lynn." I reached out to shake her hand. I took off my jacket and sat down in the chair in the corner.

Instead of going back to her paperwork, Alice wanted to fill the time chatting. I thought I might help Sam's chances and mentioned how hopeful we were about his interview. She began what sounded like a well-rehearsed presentation on what an opportunity this company was for a young pilot. Unlike other airline crews, Seaboard's flight engineers, who filled the third—and usually the most junior seat—in the cockpit, preferred to remain in their own union and position. Anyone hired as a pilot at Seaboard would fly immediately instead of waiting for years to upgrade to the copilot/first officer seat, which was customary at TWA and other airlines.

As we continued to talk, she discovered I was also a pilot, on furlough from TWA, with a college degree. She took the time to jot down notes between questions.

"Why aren't you applying too?" she asked. "If Sam is hired and goes to England to fly the DC-8, you could go along, or you could both end up working here on the 747."

With complete naïve confidence, I replied, "The TWA furlough will last only two more months. I wouldn't want to waste time training and then quit. I can keep him company better without working."

She talked patiently, as she would to a child.

"You know they always say that, don't you? Furloughs last years. Before you leave, just stop in to say hi to Captain Hirschberg." Then with a shy smile, she added, "We call him the Silver Eagle. You'll see why."

She was quite in awe of the man. I figured stopping in to show support for Sam couldn't hurt.

Sam exited the door across the hall, and I stood up to greet him. Alice rushed past me, saying, "follow me" over her shoulder and "she will be just a minute" to Sam. She opened the door Sam had just closed and motioned for me to step in. Placing some papers she carried on Captain Hirschberg's desk, she made eye contact with him, nodded, and said simply, "This is Lynn."

With a soldier's erect posture and confident steel-blue eyes that softened with his smile, he had a commanding presence even while sitting at his desk.

"Have a seat."

His voice was calm, pleasant, and more conversational than I expected. He didn't seem annoyed at all to have the end of his workday delayed. I relaxed into my chair and watched as he looked over Alice's papers. He was a strikingly handsome man in his fifties with a tanned face and thick silver hair. I could immediately understand his secretary's respect and devotion. I wondered if there might be a personal relationship as well as professional.

He looked up at me, smiling in anticipation of my reaction to the offer he was about to make. Pointing at a model of the 747 on his desk, a miniature duplicate of the one I had admired on the ramp, he said the words that changed my life.

"How would you like to be the first woman to fly the 747?"

I had no idea how to respond. I couldn't imagine why he would ask me such a thing. Was it his idea of a joke, a test? Well, I knew the correct answer and wouldn't be anyone's fool.

"Women can't fly the heavies," I stated matter-of-factly, my smile gone.

Now his smile disappeared as well. It was not the response he expected.

"What? Why not? Who told you that?"

The moment he had envisioned was ruined as I stumbled with my role and dialogue in his imagined scenario.

Was this more tests, or teasing? Or maybe he honestly didn't know.

"I worked at TWA for eight years, and the guys there told me that if two engines go out on one side, the amount of rudder pressure needed to keep the big, heavier planes like the 747 going straight is too much for a girl."

His smile was back. In fact, he was almost laughing.

"That's hogwash. It's all hydraulics. I'll show you."

He leaned forward as if inviting me along into his fantasy world. There was an energy about him that drew me in. I imagined his mind was rarely still, and it seemed having me in the 747 was what he was imagining. This was not going at all as I had expected. We were supposed to be talking about Sam and the DC-8. Trying to get us back on track and reality, I cleared my throat.

"Alice tells me the DC-8 is based in England. That's where my friend Karen is. We were roommates. I guess if Sam gets hired, I'll get to see her, too."

I wasn't sure whether he heard me. He was standing, my cue to leave. Showing me to the door, he asked the oddest question. "Have you taken the Stanine test?"

I stopped to think. It sounded familiar.

"Yes, I think so. It was a part of a United interview I did two years ago."

Two weeks later, back in Miami, the call came while Sam was out. It was Alice. The chat she and I had in her office gave her all the information she needed to fill out an application for me. She immediately approved it, and then handed it to the Silver Eagle. My meeting with Captain Hirschberg was just to make it official. Seaboard World Airlines wanted me to come work for them.

Never underestimate the power of the secretary.

The offer would have been fantastic if Sam had been hired, too. But he wasn't. He lacked a four-year degree and the Stanine test results, both of which I had. Had I hurt his chances of getting the job when I thought I was helping?

"If I say no, will Sam be hired in my place?" I asked Alice.

"No, dear. He doesn't meet the requirements. You do. Training starts on the first Monday in March, one week from today. We are so pleased to have you."

The thought of Sam's disappointment that I was hired over him—again— was more than I could bear.

"Alice, I can't. I'm engaged. It's too much to ask. I made this commitment to Sam and me first. I have to keep it."

"I won't say anything to Captain Hirschberg yet. Call me on Friday either way. Think it over."

Thinking it over was all I could do. It was the 747, my favorite airplane, everyone's favorite airplane. She could be mine for the asking, and I hadn't even asked! It seemed she wanted me. How could I pass this up? How often does your dream job come along? The universe was opening a door, offering an opportunity. Did I dare say no, not now?

But how could I give up the life I had with the man I loved? We had been together for six years, helping each other, sharing our love of flying, studying, learning, growing, living together. We knew each other better than anyone else did. I owed him for what I had accomplished and for who I had become. How could I turn my back on that? But why should I have to? If he loved me, he would want me happy, and he would be pleased for me, right? It's how I would react if things were reversed.

However, if he was upset, I could hardly blame him. He was the one who went for the interview at my urging. This was the second job he wanted that I was offered. The fact that I was the more qualified didn't seem to matter. If I were a guy friend, he would be a good sport and congratulate me. Surely, he would want to support me in my career as I would his. If he can't do that, it's good to know now. Whatever the decision, I finally concluded, hopefully, we would figure it out together.

I told Sam about the call as soon as he got home and quickly added my decision not to go, citing my loving logic. But the ensuing conversation debating our options made it clear I was in a lose/lose situation. If I didn't accept the offer, I lost his respect as a serious career pilot. If I took the job, I risked losing him, his love for me as a woman, and our life together.

All week we tried to go on as normal, but normal didn't exist anymore. We hardly spoke. It was so unfair. In those days, men didn't find themselves having to choose between personal and professional lives. He couldn't relate to my situation. I could already feel the resentment bubbling up through my ongoing inner dialogue. For a week, I held in my mind the decision to turn down the offer to see how it felt. I lived with it, put it on like a coat—a heavy coat in the Miami sun that was stifling me. I couldn't breathe. I switched to the take-the-job-decision coat and felt lighter, happier, excited. My inner debate finally culminated one day as I was vacuuming our pea-green shag rug, thinking, *I could be flying a 747.*

When Sam got home Thursday evening, I had dinner and my rehearsed talk ready. I thought we could have a calm discussion, consider the pros and cons and find ways to handle *our* decision. I introduced the subject with, "I've been thinking that I'd like to accept the Seaboard offer. Maybe down the road...."

"Of course, you have to take it," Sam interrupted. "Who could turn that down? But I'm not going to be following someone around the country for their job."

That pretty much summed it up and said it all. He walked into the kitchen with the excuse of getting a glass of water.

I didn't recognize the scowling face avoiding me. Where was the man I had come to know and love?

"I never asked you to," I said to his back, trying to calm what seemed to have suddenly escalated to an argument. "We've handled separations before. We love—"

He, too, must have had discussions within himself and with others. He interrupted me again, turning to face me and speaking quickly as if rehearsed.

"What's the point? If we get married and have kids, I want their mom home raising them, not gone on overnights. And I want her there when I come home. How would we ever see each other? That's not a marriage or a family. I thought things would eventually get better, but they're getting worse. Now you'll be flying international, maybe based in England."

He set the glass of water on the table and finally looked right at me. I could see he was hurting, and I understood his thoughts. His brothers' wives and both of our mothers, like many women, were stay-at-home moms and what he expected to have in his life. When we met, I was a flight attendant with flying as a hobby he encouraged. Flying was his future career, not mine. Now it was I who had the more successful future. Everything had changed. I also wanted a family and to be home with our children as much as possible. I thought deciding how we would make that happen was years away and something we would handle together.

"I guess I just thought somehow we'd make it all work out," I said weakly, feeling the pangs of rejection and abandonment.

"I don't see how. It hasn't worked for a while."

He left the table, his plate of food untouched. Then he quietly shared his conclusions to our situation and the next steps we would take in what was once a relationship.

"I hate goodbyes. Please take a taxi to the airport. Calling just makes it harder, so let's not."

And just like that, there was no more "we."

I had never seen his eyes unable to meet mine. He reached for his jacket and turned toward the door. He simply walked out of the door and out of my life.

I was crushed. Who was that person? What had just happened? I felt sick, trapped, homeless, hopeless, but the die was cast. I had just been handed the opportunity of a lifetime—a dream come true that I hadn't even asked for. At the same time, I watched another dream I had worked years to create crumble. I put the beautiful ring that had made me so happy on the table with the uneaten dinner. I wondered if he had already found someone else who would wear it one day. He no longer wanted me in his life, so why would I want to be there? There was no one to celebrate or cry with me as I packed.

Training started on Monday in New York. A hotel room was provided and waiting. There was every reason to go and none to stay. I prepared to catch a late flight out of Miami that night. Everything I owned still fit into two suitcases. Somehow leaving a heart behind made them feel heavier.

Before I left for the airport, I called Alice. At least one person was happy.

Section IV:

The 747 and Me

24

The Making of a 747 Pilot

The hotel was expecting me. I wondered whether Alice knew I would end up accepting the job before I did. On Monday morning, I reported to the same building at JFK where I had unintentionally interviewed. Training started immediately, but not on the 747 as I had expected. I was told I would be in ground school on the DC-8 with only one other classmate, Tim Gurney.

For the first week, I was a mess. I had a constant migraine, I was convinced I was getting an ulcer, and I found it hard to eat or sleep. Unable to leave my wound alone, I continually revisited my decision to break off my engagement, going over all the facts and options, only to come to the same conclusion. Why would I want to be where I wasn't wanted instead of where I was? Seaboard had invited me to New York to join their airline and seemed happy to have me.

Once I finally came to my senses, it occurred to me that I had won the pilot jackpot. Seaboard was the first pick of many aspiring pilots. It had the biggest and best planes, allowed the newly hired pilot to go directly to the first officer seat, and offered the best salary. I would also find it was where to find top-notch ground instructors and a chief pilot who created an atmosphere of inclusion and empathy.

And, I could not have asked for a better classmate, study-buddy, simulator partner than Tim. We were supposed to be a class of four, but one guy was a no-show, and another failed his physical, leaving just Tim and me. Flight training is an intense process, and a competent partner is crucial. Tim filled the bill. He had been flying for half his life—since he was fifteen. Like me, his experience was in civilian flying, including a Twin Otter at a commuter airline. However, he had also flown large older planes like the DC-3 and DC-8 and flown in Sri Lanka. He knew other female pilots, so I wasn't an oddity or unpleasant surprise. Tim was of average height and build with sandy hair, slightly balding. He was six months older, which put me at the bottom of the seniority list. He had tons of energy, an easy-to-like personality, and most importantly, a willingness to work together. His previous knowledge of the plane and his excellent memory helped us complete our four-week ground school program with high marks. The demanding schedule and studying were just what I needed to get my mind off Sam.

The day before we were to begin using our newly gained knowledge in the DC-8 simulator, we got word of the latest bid results. The bid allowed all the airline's pilots to choose which plane, seat, and base they preferred based on seniority. Because the pilots based on the DC-8 in London received more pay and didn't have to pay U.S. income tax because of an interpretation of tax law, the DC-8 became the senior, preferred plane. That left Tim and me at the bottom of the seniority list with what was left over—the 747 in New York! Unbelievable! (I wondered if Captain Hirschberg had known this would happen). The most senior airplane at every other airline was ours as the most junior pilots at Seaboard! We ran out onto the ramp to check out "our" new plane. The plane was shiny and new with gold leather pilot seats—where we would be sitting. We were like kids at Christmas playing in our new toy, pretending to fly. We reminded each other that our imagining could become our reality—with a lot of work.

We didn't mind starting ground school all over again with new instructors. Each system instructor was a mechanic with that system as his specialty. The instructors used the same tactile teaching method as Mr. Archibald, my teacher in Miami, and were just as dedicated. They brought in aircraft parts to help explain the systems and how everything worked as a unit.

Since Boeing stays consistent with its terminology and basic concepts, I could see how the 747 was a bigger, better, more modern version of the 727 I already knew. As the latest and most modern, her designers built on all the technology and knowledge that had gone into previous models, creating a much improved, simplified, and safer aircraft. With four engines and even more back-ups to every system, the 747 could function and safely land with only one engine working.

Tim and I marveled at all the innovations in the plane's design. The eighteen-wheel, trunked, gimbaled landing gear made landings the smoothest passengers had ever experienced. The new triple channel INS (inertial navigation system) combined with three autopilots allowed excellent navigation ability and landings to the lowest allowable minimums. The auto-land, auto roll-out, and auto-braking features seemed futuristic, capable of bringing a plane to a full stop on centerline after landing with minimal pilot input. She was a combination of modern science, technology, and beauty that I got to know inside and out.

Most pilots and passengers considered the 747 to be the Queen of the Skies, the most beautiful and safest plane ever made and the favorite at any airline with her in their fleet. However, I got to do more than just admire her beauty; I got to fly her!

The 747 was the first jet I ever flew and remained my favorite throughout my career. Although I had a steep learning curve, I thought it was the perfect place to start. The process to become a 747 pilot in 1980 included a sequence of three training and testing segments. First, there was classroom instruction to teach systems, procedure, and regulations, ending with a thorough oral exam by the FAA. That was followed by training in a simulator to demonstrate handling emergencies and abnormal situations, ending with a check ride with an FAA designee, a pilot within the airline certified by the FAA to conduct check rides for them. The final step was a check ride in the real plane with an FAA representative. Whenever I doubted my abilities along the way, I would think of the confidence Captain Hirschberg and my other instructors had shown in me and decided to trust their insight and judgment of me over my own.

After four weeks of ground school and passing written and oral exams, we were ready for simulator training. Seaboard had simulator instructors but no simulators, so they rented them from United in Denver and American in Dallas. In Denver, we got the midnight-to-four a.m. time slot, which was supposed to be divided between Tim and me. However, the Seaboard instructor brought along his nineteen-year-old son to fly half of my time with the rationale that I could learn just as much by watching. Our instructor had been the youngest pilot to be hired at Seaboard and hoped his son would continue the tradition by being ready to take the next empty spot. I tried not to take it personally or as a prediction.

Despite our instructor's outrageous attitude, we made it through a week of nightly training sessions. Tim and I took turns in the left and right seats, while our instructor ran the simulator, teaching us how to deal with all the normal, abnormal, and emergency situations in the procedures manual. We learned to fly visual and various types of instrument approaches, perform aborted takeoffs and landings, recover from unusual situations, handle system failures, enter holding patterns, and dump fuel to landing weight. We practiced stalls, steep turns, and procedures for an array of emergency and abnormal conditions that were more safely demonstrated and practiced in a simulator than in a plane.

We were nearing the end of our allotted training time when the instructor's plans literally came crashing down around him. One night, for "fun" he took over the pilot seat and tried to show us a barrel roll, which caused the simulator to jump the jacks and come loose from the hydraulic supports. The computer and the large simulator it controlled made a horrible sound as it came down hard and then lay there, silent and still. He tried to blame the girl trainee.

We headed to Dallas, where a new instructor was waiting for us to complete our training and check rides using American Airlines' simulators. John, our new instructor and check airman, would conduct the simulator portion of our check ride. Fred, a professional flight engineer, would join us to perform the F/E duties during the check ride to make it more authentic. Much of what a pilot has to demonstrate during certification is a scenario too dangerous to create intentionally in the real plane for training or testing. After some unfortunate accidents at several airlines, the FAA approved their demonstration in the simulator. The "sim ride" was the most demanding part of the validation process and what Tim and I had devoted ourselves to during the previous month.

John, a Seaboard pilot designee, had been deemed capable by the FAA to give simulator check rides. Fred was an excellent flight engineer and a welcomed addition to our check-ride crew. Under John's instruction and with Fred's support, Tim and I spent four grueling hours performing steep turns, stalls, precision and non-precision approaches, missed approaches, engine failures or fires during takeoff, three-engine approaches resulting in a go-around or a full-stop landing, while never knowing what would happen next.

Our time spent studying, the effort we put into training, and all the practice paid off. Pleased with our performance, John congratulated us on passing this portion of the testing process. He predicted we would have no problem completing the final check ride step in the real plane. The adrenaline-pumping experience left us elated, sweating, and exhausted. We made plans to celebrate officially later that evening.

As we were leaving the sim building, Captain Hirschberg was entering. Although his job as Seaboard's VP of flight operations was at a desk, he liked to fly an occasional trip as a captain. When we stopped to chat, he explained that he was taking advantage of having the simulator and a check airman available for his PC—a pilot check required every six months to fly legally.

He addressed John with a smile.

"From the looks on everyone's faces, I assume all went well?"

"They did great," John responded for us while Fred nodded in agreement.

"Good," said Captain Hirschberg, and then surprised me with, "I need someone in the right seat for my ride. Lynn, would you have time?"

I didn't consider it a question. What else but "yes" would I say to the man I had to thank for my incredible job?

"Sure," I said. "Right after a bathroom stop." Flying can be brutal on the bladder. I also needed to walk around a bit to offset the adrenaline rushing through my system and the ache in my leg from holding in rudder pressure for the engine-out procedures.

I walked with Tim to the building exit, wanting a chance to savor our shared victory. Neither of us could stop smiling as we recounted the highlights of the ride and finally ended with a big hug—maybe not professional, and too girly, but it was a special occasion. Tim didn't seem to mind. He waved as he walked away.

"Have fun flying with Captain H. I hear he's amazing. See ya back at the ranch."

I found John, Fred, and Captain Hirschberg chatting comfortably while waiting for me to take my place in the right seat and prepare my panel.

After a week in the simulator with Tim, I was well versed in my duties as a first officer and could support Captain Hirschberg from the right seat as he performed all the required maneuvers. Tim was right. Captain H was one of the best pilots, instructors, and people I ever met. Always in control, never surprised or flustered, he made flying look so natural and easy. I watched every move, wanting to be like him.

As he talked through his actions and thought process, I watched him set the throttles at selected power settings at the beginning of the descent to an approach and not have to touch them again until landing. The extension of flaps and gear at the correct time decreased the speed gradually and smoothly to touchdown. He made the approach to a runway a sporting experience, like a perfect ski run, NASCAR lap, or barrel-racing ride. Each turn and movement had minimum effort with maximum effect.

Captain Hirschberg used the auto-land system to teach landing the huge plane smoothly. He instructed me to hold the yoke and throttles lightly as the auto-pilot made a perfect landing. I felt and watched the plane flare, its huge nose rise, one and one-half degrees at fifty-three feet and the thrust levers come to idle at thirty-five feet. With adjustments for variations in weight, he said it worked every time. I paid attention to his every word and action and was sorry when we finished in record time. It's a rare treat to get to watch a pro at work, especially one so willing to teach.

After the last landing, instead of unbuckling and leaving his seat, he turned to me.

"I think we still have some time. If John and Fred don't mind, do you want to show me what you've learned?"

Again, what could I say but, "Sure."

John and Fred didn't mind at all. They quickly set the simulator for takeoff. I took up the now-familiar position with my right hand on the yoke and the fingers of my left hand settled into the indentations of the four engines' throttles. I loved the feeling of pushing those throttles forward and feeling the enormous machine's response. The engines roared to life, and we were racing down the runway. My reverie and feeling of oneness with the machine were short-lived.

"Engine failure, number four," Captain Hirschberg declared.

We were past V1 speed, going too fast to stop before the end of the runway. Red warning lights flashed on the cockpit panel as the huge plane veered off centerline. I immediately pushed hard on the rudder pedal to bring the jumbo jet's nose back to the wide white stripe. With two engines at full takeoff power on one side and only one on the other, it took all the strength I could summon to keep us going straight. Continuing to correct for the uneven thrust, I pulled back on the yoke to leave the runway and lift the big jet into the air.

As we climbed, I called for the gear to be retracted and asked Fred to add rudder trim, relieving some of the pressure on my leg. At eight hundred feet, I released the back pressure on the yoke to cause the plane's nose to fall slightly, reduce the climb, and accelerate to maneuvering speed.

"Set max continuous thrust. Bring flaps to 10 degrees. Tell tower we had an engine failure and want a straight-out departure. We need to return and want the longest runway in use. And start the engine failure/fire checklist." I spoke to Captain Hirschberg while willing the instruments in front of me to settle down.

At our assigned altitude, I reduced the power and complied with the checklist items as Captain Hirschberg read them. With the situation under control, we turned to the runway, and configured for landing. I was about to call for landing flaps when Captain Hirshberg called out another warning.

"Truck on the runway! Go around!"

This second alert surprised me so much that I contradicted him.

"No there's not," I objected, thinking this was more of a demonstration than I was expecting.

"Wrong response. Yes, there is. Go around."

I pushed the throttles to near max power, compensating for the uneven thrust by pushing hard on the rudder pedal, and executed the go-around.

"Tell tower we are on the missed and will be returning—again," I ordered through clenched teeth as I flew the go-around procedure.

We were on the downwind leg, setting up for the approach to land, when I got the next surprise.

"Engine failure. Number three," Fred called out as Captain Hirschberg pulled the second throttle to idle on the same side as the one that was already dead. Suddenly, I felt the power change, needing even more rudder to go straight. Warning indicator lights lit up and dials moved, confirming that another engine was now useless.

Damn, I thought. *Why would he do this to me?*

Anger and adrenaline surged strength into my leg to help take the rudder pedal nearly to the floor as I kept the huge plane on the same heading. I had to lock my knee and brace myself against the back of my seat until we began descending, when I could decrease the power and ease off the rudder pressure a bit. I began yet another approach in an abnormal configuration.

By the time we were on final, and I was calling out "gear down," my voice and leg were shaking from exhaustion, irritation, frustration. I knew this scenario had never happened in a real 747 and did not have to be demonstrated on a first officer's check ride.

I put my arguments away and concentrated on setting the power correctly for only two engines. Again, I configured the plane for landing, following the instruments that led me down the glideslope to the runway.

Captain Hirshberg's words in training—"small movements and changes"—replayed in my mind as I struggled to stay on course. Small course and power corrections minimized rudder input changes and prevented a cycle of overcorrections. The approach and landing went well. Not perfect, but well within parameters. Sometimes that's the definition of a good landing—no blood or bent metal.

I put the anger and frustration I was feeling aside, as we put the plane to bed. John and Fred congratulated me on an excellent job and a fun evening, promising to meet us for a celebratory dinner. Pilots have a strange definition of "fun."

I waited until I was alone with my so-called mentor. I stared straight ahead, refusing to face the man I so hoped to please.

"Why on earth would you do that to me?" I asked Captain Hirschberg in a measured, angry tone. "Two engines out? Same side?

"I'm not having you up there thinking you can't do something you can," he said calmly, smiling at me with fatherly affection. "You're welcome. Next time use more rudder trim."

I remembered the day we met when I declared to him that women weren't strong enough to fly the heavies. All he said that day was, "I'll show you." And he did. He had put me in the very situation I had been told for so many years that a woman couldn't handle. He wanted me to have the confidence in myself that he had in me.

"Oh. Well, then, thank you," I stammered, as gratitude quickly replaced my anger.

After the simulator, my final check ride was in the plane with the FAA watching. The jumbo jet's only occupants that evening were FAA inspector Bill Bumpus, Captain Hirschberg, flight engineer Fred, Tim, and me. We took off at sunset with a pastel sky as a backdrop to the city's darkened skyline. Departing JFK, we flew south to the airport in Atlantic City, where there were fewer planes and more space. There, we would have plenty of room for the challenging maneuvers of the exam. Mr. Bumpus gladly accepted Captain Hirschberg's invitation to have the fun of flying us there.

Tim and I sat in the back of the upper deck, trying to relax on lounge seats. The plane we were flying could be converted from carrying cargo to passengers. The galley had been fully catered for dinner, but I was too nervous to eat. This was the final step before declaring us 747 pilots.

The FAA exam required that we fly visual and instrument approaches with all four engines working and with an engine disabled. We had to demonstrate our ability to do full-stop landings and go-around procedures for aborted landings. We had practiced everything multiple times in the simulator, but this was the real thing. We were flying a real 747! Our imagining that evening on the ramp when we learned that we would fly the 747 had become our latest reality.

It was time to show the FAA all we had learned.

Tim went first and did great. After a grueling two hours in the hot seat, he finished, and it was my turn. There had been no surprises, and everyone was pleased with his performance. I only hoped I would fare as well.

I wasn't sure when the warm-up stopped and the check-ride began during my two-hour demonstration as a 747 pilot. I just complied with the demands to perform maneuvers and instrument approaches, staying focused on the immediate situation. There was no time to worry about what would happen next or mentally replay anything that had happened before. I wore a hood that prevented me from seeing outside—I had to rely solely on the array of instruments on the dashboard. Captain Hirschberg performed the duties of my copilot flawlessly. All went as rehearsed. I "lost an engine" during the last takeoff. That led to the three-engine approach, which led to a three-engine go-around, and finally an approach to a full-stop landing. I thought it all went pretty well. Certainly not as precise as Captain Hirschberg's flying or as confident as Tim, but I hoped it was good enough.

I wasn't quite sure what Mr. Bumpus meant when he said, "Okay. That's enough," after my last landing. There were so many ways to take that, so many interpretations of "enough."

As I got out of my seat, I had to ask, "Enough because it was good enough—or you couldn't take anymore?"

He thought I was joking and laughed.

"You both did great. Go relax. Carl is itching to get his hands on the controls to take us home."

Captain Hirschberg did just that as I joined Tim in the lounge for the ride home. We found some ginger ale to toast our success. The months of classes, tests, oral exam, simulator training, and check ride, culminating in the final "real plane" check ride, was over. We did it! The day we first sat in the cockpit, imagining we were flying the plane, had become a reality. We were 747 pilots!

After Captain Hirshberg instilled the self-confidence I needed in my capability, he turned to building my confidence in the machine. He chose a D-check in Tulsa for that experience.

Planes are continually put through different levels of inspections and checks to maintain and ensure their airworthiness. The D-check is the most extensive and is frequently performed after a major overhaul. During that test flight, the plane is purposefully flown to its literal limits to ensure all the warning systems function correctly.

I was allowed to conduct the D-check and take a 747 to the limits! Captain Hirschberg was in the left seat and a mechanic holding a clipboard sat on the jumpseat. As the mechanic issued instructions, it was my job to perform the actions that would trigger the warnings as he checked them off and made notes. We did steep turns, dives and climbs, and stalls in every configuration to check red-line limits, aural warnings, and physical indicators. It was amazing to see and feel something that huge be so responsive and graceful, even in the worst conditions.

To check the stall warning system, I was instructed to pull back on the yoke to keep the nose up. The plane slowed, and the wind over the wing stalled, reducing the airflow necessary for lift and flight. The warnings sounded—first a horn, then a clacker, and ultimately the stick shaker. Over the racket, the guy with the clipboard yelled, "Let go!"

I simply let go of the yoke and watched in awe as her nose came down to allow the wind to flow evenly over her wings again, without falling off to one side or the other, catching herself as if on a cloud, gliding into silent recovery—until we did it again—and again—and again. It was the same amazing experience in every configuration with flap and gear down or up, in turns or straight. The steep turns were the most fun. I was surprised at the amount of thrust and back pressure on the yoke needed to keep altitude. It was the only time and place I'd be allowed to bank a commercial jet past the red line while listening to the recorded voice admonishing me with "BANK ANGLE BANK ANGLE" over and over until I corrected. Approaching the ground too fast caused the same voice to tell me "SINK RATE WHOOP WHOOP PULL UP SINK RATE WHOOP WHOOP PULL UP ."

I couldn't remember ever having so much fun. I was in awe of the capability and safety margins built into the machine. I was disappointed when the guy with the clipboard finally said, "Okay, that's everything." It felt a bit strange to return to just flying normally.

Captain Hirschberg's, "I've got it," took me by surprise. With a smile of thanks, I took my hands off the yoke. The bonding experience left me with the utmost confidence in the beautiful machine, which I'm sure was his intent, while showing both of us what I could handle.

As he flew us in for landing, I had time to reflect on the message I was continually being given. *I could do this.* All of the negative comments saying otherwise were wrong. I had proven it to myself. Now I could prove it to the world.

Seaboard World Airlines 747 Containership
Courtesy of Boeing Co.

25

A Perfect Day

Completing the months of training and testing satisfied all the FAA's requirements, but the airline still needed us to jump through some hoops of their own making. Before we could be welcomed into the Seaboard family and turned over to scheduling for assigned trips, we needed to complete IOE (Initial Operating Experience) or line qualification, flying under the supervision of an experienced training captain, called a line check airman. Since Seaboard flew domestic and international routes, I had to be qualified on both. My two-day international IOE was to Dover, Frankfurt, Madrid, and back to JFK. I had one day to rest, then flew a domestic trip from JFK to Chicago, San Francisco, Los Angeles, Chicago, and back to JFK, also in two days.

For my new job, I needed to learn to sleep during the day and be awake at night to fly on "the dark side of the clock." Cargo planes often fly at night. The evening air is cooler, which gives the plane better performance and uses less fuel. The airport isn't as busy, so time isn't wasted waiting for takeoff and landing. Landing fees are lower, airways less crowded, and cargo doesn't care when it travels. I didn't mind either. Stars and constellations above and lights outlining the coastlines and cities below made for spectacular views.

With IOEs out of the way, I was ready for my first official flight as a 747 pilot on July 7, 1980. Captain Hirschberg chose to fly as my captain. He also decided to have the event of the first woman to fly a 747 commemorated with photographs and interviews.

At first, I didn't appreciate all the attention. I had done very well through training, but what if I messed up? There was no other female pilot to tell me I could do this because they or someone else had. I was nervous enough. I didn't want the added stress of makeup, hairstyle, posing, finding the right words to express how I felt. But mainly, I didn't want my peers watching me get special treatment and attention as I was trying to fit in. However, now I'm glad Captain Hirschberg got his way. I love the photos capturing one of the most significant events in my career. Years later one was placed in the Smithsonian along with my uniform.

For my first official flight, Captain Hirschberg chose a coast-to-coast flight with stops in Chicago and San Francisco on the way to Los Angeles, our final destination. We were flying in and out of some of the busiest airports in the country. We always added "heavy" to the end of our call sign, which identifies an aircraft weighing more than 300,000 pounds, as a courtesy to other aircraft and notice to the controller. Other planes needed extra room behind the 747 because of the powerful wake it created. Following too close behind could create a turbulent ride in other jets and be disastrous for small aircraft.

We had perfect summer weather for our three-day, two-night trip. Usually, the two flying pilots take turns at the helm and on the radios, but Captain Hirschberg allowed me to do all the flying!

At each station, he introduced me to the station manager, dispatcher, and maintenance manager. These were the people I would work with while on the ground at their city's airport. The dispatcher would have ready the latest weather, flight plan, and any other information pertinent to the flight. The maintenance guys were available to perform the routine checks and to address any write-ups put in the maintenance log. The station manager made sure everything ran smoothly and was the person to go to if it didn't. Everyone was very welcoming and offered their assistance if I needed it in the future. My mentor was doing all he could to make my entry into new territory as smooth as possible for everyone. Knowing I had his confidence and support made all the difference in the world.

Throughout the flight, I was included in every decision that arose. The captain has the final say, but a good one will ask the crew for input to get the most information possible. The discussion also makes an excellent teaching opportunity for the less-experienced pilots. Captain Hirschberg was not only helping me to become a good first officer, but he was also setting the example I would follow when I became a captain. Thanks to him, I loved the plane and my job. I was just twenty-nine, and I had reached the position most pilots strive for over an entire career. And the view was great!

The scenery on our coast-to-coast flights was spectacular from seven miles up in the sky. I could imagine settlers heading west in their wagon trains from the colonies, venturing into the Midwest with its fertile valleys, forests, and the wide Mississippi River. I wondered what it must have been like crossing the empty plains, the deserts, finding a pass through the Rocky Mountains, and coming upon the Grand Canyon. What a sight it must have been for those strong and determined enough to continue until the Pacific Ocean came into view.

However, with all the stops and new information to absorb, there wasn't much time at altitude to relax and enjoy the scenery. Captain Hirshberg used the time to teach me all he could about the plane and my new role. It was a constant learning experience. A major part of my job as first officer was navigation. In the days before GPS, we had to rely on more primitive systems.

Seaboard's 747s had the latest technology for its day. On domestic routes, we flew on assigned airways defined by ground-based navigational aids and at an altitude that kept us clear of other traffic. On the transatlantic routes, there were no ground-based aids, of course, so the plane used INS—Inertial Navigation System. Spinning gyroscopes sensed the plane's movements on the three axes and were able to tell the pilots where they were. While at the gate, it was my job to enter the plane's exact position into the computer in longitude and latitude. It was crucial that I got it correct. As the plane moved, the gyros sensed movement in three dimensions and sent a read-out to a display in the cockpit. While crossing the ocean, INS readings were taken every forty-five minutes. Our position was reported to Oceanic Control and marked with an X on the navigation chart. Designated altitudes for traffic going in the same direction, separation by two thousand feet from opposite-direction traffic, plus in-trail spacing, maintained a safe distance between aircraft in flight. Adhering to the flight plan and reporting one's position allowed the system to work smoothly and safely. It also allowed officials to know the plane's last reported location if an emergency occurred.

I soaked up everything my chief pilot could tell me as he made sure I was not only well-trained but also well-accepted at his airline. On my first day, we logged over eight hours of flight time plus another six on the ground. A fourteen-hour workday was not unusual for a cargo pilot. By flying west, we had the bonus of extra hours of summer sunlight.

We arrived at our destination, Los Angeles, landing on 25R as the sun sank below the Pacific at the end of the runway. It was a perfect end to a perfect day—my first day as a 747 pilot.

Checking in for Seaboard World 747 flight

In first officer seat

First Flight as 747 pilot

26

From Dream to Reality

Following Captain Hirschberg's personal introduction to the airline's system, I was made available to scheduling. Once again, I found myself on the bottom of an airline seniority list as the most junior pilot and on reserve. I had to stay available to be sent anywhere at any time, but I had no complaints. With a variety of destinations, flight details, and crew members, every trip was a new, exciting experience.

As first officer, the captain and I alternated flying and non-flying duties. When I wasn't flying, I was responsible for communication and navigation, while the flight engineer took care of the aircraft systems at his panel. Although we each had our specific roles, we were continually double-checking to be aware of everything going on in the cockpit.

Seaboard was unique among the airlines in not requiring their flight engineers to become pilots or part of the pilot union. These flight engineers would never upgrade to a flying seat and didn't have to retire at age sixty as the pilots did. Some pilots transitioned to the flight engineer seat after their mandatory retirement. Consequently, on my flights, the flight engineer was often older than the captain, and both were a generation older than I. This arrangement made it easy to fall into the role of daughter or eager student to create a comfortable work environment. Possibly thanks to the example set by Captain Hirschberg, my fellow crewmembers were respectful and didn't seem to mind my arrival at all. They were a laid-back group who didn't seem to mind much of anything. Most were without college degrees and joked that if not for WWII, they'd be in a different eighteen-wheeler, since both a semi-trailer truck and the 747 have eighteen wheels. The strong, silent type, these guys didn't initiate much conversation. I didn't take it personally, assuming they were that way with everyone.

There was another reason for the quiet cockpit—someone was usually sleeping. We took off when most people were going to bed. The captain's briefing always included clarifying the order in which we could nap after we leveled off at flight altitude with autopilot on, route confirmed, and no immediate concerns. It had to be planned so that two people were always alert in the cockpit. The standing joke was, "I better not wake up and find you sleeping." No one minded another closing their eyes; they just had to announce it. This practice made for an alert, rested crew on landing eight to twelve hours later when full attention was needed. It made complete sense to me. Years later, the FAA finally recommended it.

I didn't mind the cockpit silence, broken only by required radio calls and position reports. Miles above the planet with a 180-degree panoramic view of creation is a great place to think, dream, meditate, check in with God. The scene outside our windshield was constantly changing. Rivers and fields, mountain ranges and coastlines came into view. On our ocean crossings, I thought of the men and women who made the dangerous sea voyage in vessels that took months or years that we could now travel in comfort in a few hours. Cloud formations, lightning storms, constellations, sun and moon risings and settings offered a spectacular show. The experience was as close to becoming one with the wind and sky as humanly possible.

One particular night crossing is etched in my memory. An older, crusty captain who spoke only when absolutely necessary and never made eye contact was at the helm. It was a gorgeous, clear, moonless night, which allowed the stars to shine all the brighter. Heading east after leaving JFK and nearing the PNR (point of no return), city lights along the Eastern Seaboard were behind us, and only the darkness of the ocean lay below. I noticed a tiny pinpoint of light straight ahead. I thought it might be another plane in the far distant sky or a ship on the ocean below. As I watched it get bigger, light emanated from its sides, creating a line that defined the water from the space above. The line of light was red at the bottom, then gradually melded into orange, yellow, and finally, a white glow. The round source of light became more prominent, and the lines grew longer and wider, stretching out on both sides to wrap around us. From this glowing orb directly in front came a ribbon of light glistening on the surface below, reaching toward us, seeming to invite us, leading us toward it. It was the rising full moon!

We flew over the wavy liquid light, a path of mercury, leading to the horizon where the moon continued to rise from the sea and light the night sky. Like Dorothy and friends following the yellow brick road to Oz, my crew and I traveled the shimmering road below toward the horizon. The sky was so clear, the sea so calm, that from our position far above the earth, we were flying over a ribbon of moonlight.

"Wow!" was all I could say.

Even my crusty captain couldn't keep silent.

"After all this time, you think you've seen it all. Then something like this...."

He shook his head, and I thought I saw just a bit of a smile with a touch of awe.

I sat in silence, the cockpit lit with the dim lights of the instrument panel and the full moon growing in front of us. The huge orb pulled us closer as we glided east over the spectacular path of silver light. There are times in life that you know will stick with you forever. This was one of them.

I thought of all that had happened to bring me to this moment, to witness this amazing scene. I remembered pretending to float on a winged horse over a green valley, soloing in a seaplane over Lake Champlain, giving lessons and flying charters over the Everglades, flying over Midwest fields at Air Illinois, transferring from the cabin to the cockpit at TWA, and finally, soaring through the night sky over a stream of liquid mercury as a 747 pilot.

My dream had become reality. I couldn't help but wonder what adventures lay ahead.

MORE FROM CAPTAIN RIPPELMEYER

Life Takes Wings is followed by its sequel, *Life Takes Flight*, which includes more of Lynn's aviation career as she advances to captain and navigates turbulent times in her personal life and in the airline industry.

From meeting British royalty and sending her historical uniform to the Smithsonian Museum to being a *Jeopardy!* answer, Lynn's inspiring life continues to unfold in amazing ways!

Visit www.LynnRippelmeyer.com to see her on the BBC Special: *Reaching for the Skies* and learn more about the next book and its author.

To contact Captain Rippelmeyer or to invite her to speak to your group, organization, or company, complete the form on the website.

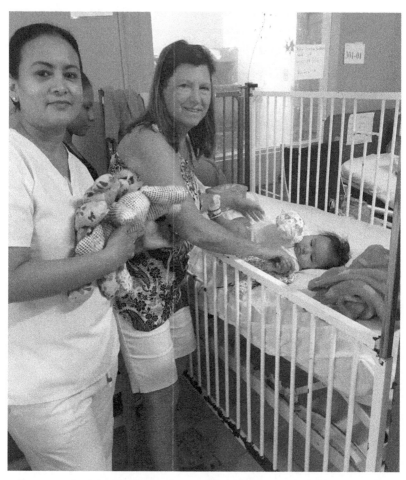

Captain Lynn Rippelmeyer created ROSE, Roatan Support Effort to aid the disadvantaged people of Roatan Island, Honduras. She transports supplies for the youth soccer league, the hospital and clinics, schools, community kitchen, and animal shelter. ROSE also coordinates with the island NGO Because We Care to give direct aid to the neediest families. Proceeds from her books help ROSE and the people of Roatan, Honduras. More information is available at www.RoatanSupportEffort.org Tax ID #82-2798779

Roatan Youth Soccer League supported by Lynn's charity, ROSE

ABOUT THE AUTHOR

Captain Lynn Rippelmeyer of Houston, Texas was the first woman to pilot the revolutionary Boeing 747 aircraft and holds a number of other firsts in aviation history, including being a member of the first all-female crew and the first person to captain a 747 Transoceanic flight. Inspired by correspondence with Jonathan Livingston Seagull author Richard Bach, she pursued her dream to be a pilot while working for TWA  as a flight attendant, leading her to another first—the first flight attendant to become a commercial airline pilot. Her uniform is part of the Smithsonian Air and Space Museum, and Alex Trebek knew her as a *Jeopardy!* answer. She has been honored by British royalty as a 'Woman of the Year' and featured in numerous television shows and specials including the BBC's *Reach for the Skies: The Adventures of Flight,* PBS's *We'll Meet Again, Working Women,* and *Inside Mighty Machines.* Lynn's experiences as a Boeing747 pilot and captain have also been published in *Women Who Fly* from the International Society of Women Airline Pilots.

A free ebook edition is available with the purchase of this book.

To claim your free ebook edition:

1. Visit MorganJamesBOGO.com
2. Sign your name CLEARLY in the space
3. Complete the form and submit a photo of the entire copyright page
4. You or your friend can download the ebook to your preferred device

Print & Digital Together Forever.

Snap a photo

Free ebook

Read anywhere